how dogs learn

how dogs learn

Mary R. Burch, Ph.D. and
Jon S. Bailey, Ph.D.

HOWELL
BOOK
HOUSE

Howell Book House
A Pearson Education Macmillan Company
1633 Broadway
New York, NY 10019

MACMILLAN is a registered trademark of Macmillan USA

Library of Congress Cataloging-in-Publication Data:

Burch, Mary R.
    How dogs learn / Mary R. Burch and Jon S. Bailey
        p.   cm.
    Includes bibliographical references and index.
    ISBN 0-87605-371-1
    1. Dogs—Training.   2. Dogs—Behavior.   I.Bailey, Jon S.
    II.Title.
    SF431.B928   1999
    636.7'08'35—dc21   98-42760
                                                CIP

Manufactured in the United States of America

10 9 8 7 6 5 4 3

Book Design: George McKeon
Cover Design: Michael J. Freeland

dedication

For Laddie,
who introduced us to dog training and changed our lives

acknowledgements

· ·

We thought when we started this book that between the two of us, we knew everything we needed to know in order to write a basic book on operant conditioning for dog training. Not long after we began writing, we discovered that a great deal of the popular literature on training dogs is full of mythology and pseudoscience. As operant conditioning has become more popular, an increasing number of trainers have attempted to teach the concepts. Some trainers combine science with their own theories. The result is that many procedures are recommended that cannot be used reliably by a variety of trainers and dogs.

We hope this book will shed some light on the subject.

We would like to gratefully acknowledge several individuals for their valuable input.

Marge Gibbs of Leash and Collar Dog Training in Lincolnshire, Illinois, provided insightful information pertaining to the behavior of dog owners, and she was a source of encouragement throughout the writing process.

Steve Lindsay of Canine Behavioral Services in Philadelphia, Pennsylvania, directed the authors to the early writing of well-known obedience trainers, and his interpretation of trends in dog training today was extremely valuable.

Mike Rashotte, Ph.D., Professor of Psychology at Florida State University, guided us to some of the critical studies in animal learning research that provide the experimental analysis of procedures equivalent to modern-day trends such as jackpotting.

In particular, we would like to thank Dr. Jack Michael at Western Michigan University for his thoughtful and detailed analysis and critique of an earlier version of this manuscript. His knowledge of the history of operant conditioning and his ability to discern subtleties and nuances of meaning and procedure are without peer in the field. We are honored that he has provided the foreword for our book.

contents

list of charts

foreword

· ·

The alliance of the practical art of animal training with the science of behavior is relatively recent. Of course, animal trainers must always have been somewhat familiar with the concepts and principles of the science of behavior, or they could not have developed the useful or entertaining behavior of their animals. And behavior scientists have long studied animal behavior as a part of their science. But relating the practical tools of animal trainers to the science of behavior nevertheless results in some clear gains for both fields.

Scientists gain another area of application in which the adequacy of existing knowledge can be evaluated, and from which new lines of scientific investigation will emerge when existing knowledge proves insufficient. Trainers gain by having their many techniques and rules integrated into a coherent system consisting of a small number of basic concepts and principles that serve as the basis for a larger number of derived relationships. Such integrated knowledge is easier to learn, easier to teach and easier to apply consistently.

Discovering failures in the fit between practice and science is also of value. Rules and practices of questionable scientific status are likely to be false rules, or they may suggest instances where our existing scientific knowledge is insufficient. Also, scientific knowledge that is not currently a part of the trainer's technology may form a basis for new practical applications.

In some respects, the main topic of Mary Burch and Jon Bailey's book is the use of rewards or reinforcers. There is no doubt that professional animal trainers are generally well aware of the importance of rewards in their training. But because the concept is familiar, there is some tendency for it to be oversimplified. The readers of this book may be surprised at the complexity, or better, the richness of the subject matter involving rewards. Well covered are the differences between primary and secondary reinforcement, between positive and negative reinforcement, and also the vexing and easily confused distinction between negative reinforcement and punishment. The sensitivity of behavior to the relation between rewards and the context in which the rewards occur (stimulus control) is also well covered; as is the sensitivity of behavior to the relation between reward availability, the passage of time, and the occurrence of previous unrewarded responses (schedules of reinforcement). The variables that alter the effectiveness of rewards, and subsequently alter the probability that the rewarded behavior will actually occur—that is, the topic of motivation—are also given careful and thorough treatment.

Especially useful to the trainer, I think, is Burch and Bailey's evenhanded and careful coverage of punishment, a topic that is seldom dealt with adequately in popular presentations of behavioral science. Because this topic, more than any other, raises ethical issues, and because the main message is often an admonition against excessive use or any use of physical punishment, the realities and complexities of this very important variable are often neglected. The fact is, many environmental changes that do not in any way involve physical pain function as forms of punishment, in the sense that they decrease the behavior that preceded them. This means a great many events affecting both trainees and trainers function as punishment. It is a topic that is just as complex as reinforcement, and must be as well understood by trainers, and by dog owners in general, if they wish to effectively understand behavior.

Another outstanding feature of this book is its coverage of factors that can strongly affect behavior but are not related to reinforcement or punishment—not even to learning—and are the results of medical conditions, genetic background, physical features of the environment and other things. The material dealt with in the section on behavioral diagnostics has only recently begun to receive appropriate consideration in applications involving human behavior problems. The animal trainer studying this book will be well ahead of many behavioral practitioners working with humans, with respect to these very important but often overlooked causes of behavioral excesses or deficits.

This book can be used in several ways. Trainers can simply study the book the same way they study any of the technical works in their field. It can also function as a handbook, where subjects can be looked up as new or puzzling situations arise. For this second use, it should be on every animal trainer's bookshelf for future reference. The book would be excellent for informal group study, with a chapter or two being the basis for discussion as part of a monthly professional meeting of trainers.

The book could also function as the substance of a formal workshop or course. In many respects, this book covers the content of an undergraduate course in learning and behavior, but with most of the examples taken from dog training. In fact, a person who mastered the material in this book would have a better start in my junior-level course on learning and motivation than the usual students who come into the course after several other undergraduate courses!

If I had to characterize this book with a single sentence, I would say that it is practically very useful without sacrificing scientific and technical accuracy.

Jack Michael, Ph.D.
Department of Psychology
Western Michigan University

introduction

In the past few decades, there has been an exciting new development in dog training: the arrival of the sophisticated trainer. Most competent, modern-day dog trainers aren't happy anymore with simply training dogs. They want to know how dogs learn, as well as how and why they behave and respond to specific learning situations.

The people whose dogs they train want to better understand their dogs, as well, so they can take their training to a higher level and communicate more clearly with their dogs.

Today's trainers and dog owners are buying books, going to seminars, joining dog training clubs, participating in dog training discussions on the Internet, subscribing to training magazines and joining professional organizations that can teach them about the science that underlies the principles of animal training.

Operant conditioning is the part of the science of behavior that explains the functional relationship between environmental events and behavior. It is a key component in explaining how all organisms (including dogs) learn.

This science is called *operant conditioning,* and this book has been written to provide dog trainers and owners with an explanation of the scientific principles behind how dogs learn.

Operant conditioning is a very important part of the science of behavior. While its applications in dog training may be newly appreciated, it is not an entirely new concept. Behavioral scientists have been studying the field since 1938, when B.F. Skinner published his landmark scientific work *The Behavior of Organisms*.

For decades, as the operant conditioning researchers developed and tested theories in their labs, animal trainers were busy out in the real world teaching animals new skills in applied settings. These trainers were often completely unaware that there was a science related to what they were doing. This science could both describe what was happening in training sessions and provide a way to make training more effective.

Historically, the development of the science and theories of operant conditioning by researchers and the practical development of new procedures by animal trainers moved forward along parallel lines. These lines finally crossed in the 1940s when scientists got involved in training animals for military use and animal entertainment acts.

By the 1980s, operant conditioning was receiving attention in a variety of animal training settings. Thousands of dog trainers had discovered there was a science that could predict how dogs would behave in certain situations. They began using the language of the science and attempting to apply its principles in training settings.

Because the current interest in operant conditioning is so great, there is a need for a book that is understandable, yet scientifically accurate. When we started writing this book, we discovered that a great deal of the popular literature related to training dogs is full of mythology and pseudoscience. The fact is, the real science is fascinating enough on its own.

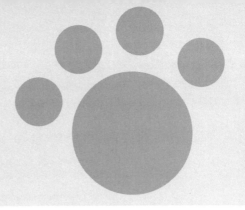

Part One

a history of animal training

When we look forward to the future of dog training, it's also very useful to look back and see where we've been. Although dog training has changed enormously in recent decades, the early trainers played a critical role in developing the world of dog training as we know it today. Understanding these trainers, and the scientific principles they were learning from, helps us understand how we ended up where we are today.

Chapter 1

the scientists

....

How operant conditioning developed in the lab

Beginning in the 1800s, behavioral scientists were in their labs discovering the principles that laid the groundwork for the 1938 arrival of operant conditioning. At the same time, without using the technical terminology or being aware of the scientific theories, dog trainers were using many operant conditioning methods. We'll look at what the scientists were doing in this chapter, and what the dog trainers were up to in the next.

DOES THE NAME PAVLOV RING A BELL?

Modern theories of behavior began with the work of Ivan Pavlov (1849–1936). A Nobel Prize winner, Pavlov was a Russian physiologist who studied digestion in dogs. In the course of his research, Pavlov observed that the dogs he was studying would salivate before food was placed in their mouths. He thought the dogs were associating the lab assistants or the sound of the door opening with food. He tested this theory by ringing a bell just before feeding the dogs. After a number of trials, ringing the bell caused the dogs to salivate.

Pavlov's work in *classical* or *respondent conditioning* explains reflexive behavior, like salivation. It does not explain voluntary behaviors.

Salivation, in Pavlov's model, is called a *conditioned reflex*. The development of such reflexes has come to be called *Pavlovian conditioning* or *classical conditioning* (we'll discuss

3

this topice in more detail in Chapter 7). Pavlov's work, also referred to as *respondent conditioning* (which means it deals with reflexes), came before operant conditioning. His theories explain why a dog begins to salivate when a food dish is rattled or its owner carries the dog food bag to the feeding area.

THORNDIKE'S LAW OF EFFECT

While Pavlov was busy in Russia studying the kind of learning that involves reflexive responses, in the United States Edward Lee Thorndike (1874–1949) began studying the effects that different consequences have on new behaviors. This was important groundwork for the development of

operant conditioning. Thorndike is known for the Law of Effect, which basically says that responses that produce rewards will tend to increase in frequency. In other words, if you do something that

Thorndike's *Law of Effect* says responses that produce rewards tend to increase in frequency.

brings you a reward, you're likely to do it again.

In one study, Thorndike placed a hungry cat in a box and recorded the amount of time it took the cat to remove a barrier to get out of the box. He then placed some food outside the box and discovered that eventually it took less time for the cat to remove the barrier. The food was an incentive, and the cat figured out the task faster and faster. Thorndike's work in the 1800s provided the foundation for all of the treat training we use with dogs today.

WATSON'S LITTLE ALBERT

J.B. Watson (1878–1958) was a psychologist who worked at Johns Hopkins University and the University of Chicago. He is credited as the father of modern behaviorism. At a time when not much was known about ways to change behavior, Watson emphasized the need to get away from concentrating on thoughts and feelings and to move toward the scientific, experimental study of behavior.

Watson conducted a well-known study with an 11-month-old boy named Albert. This study is sometimes referred to as the Little Albert study. Watson and his colleague, R. Rayner, conditioned a fear reaction in Albert. Initially, Albert was allowed to play freely with a white rat. Then, a loud noise was presented whenever Albert reached out and touched the rat. The noise was loud enough to startle Albert. In one week, whenever the rat was presented Albert would cry, even without the noise. He also generalized his fear to other things, including a dog, a rabbit and a Santa Claus mask. Watson used respondent conditioning (in this case, the startle reflex) to modify Albert's behavior.

Behaviorism is the science of behavior, while **operant conditioning** is one part of behaviorism that can be used to explain the relationship between environmental events and actions.

Watson's work can help dog trainers understand what has happened when they are dealing with extremely fearful dogs. Watson is the person who started the movement in psychology that is called *behaviorism*.

SKINNER AND OPERANT CONDITIONING

B.F. Skinner (1904–1990) was influenced by both Pavlov and Watson. He expanded Watson's work on behaviorism when he described the science of operant conditioning. When he was a doctoral student at Harvard

B.F. Skinner was influenced by the writing of Francis Bacon and the work of Charles Darwin.

University, Skinner discovered that he could systematically change the behavior of rats by giving the rats a food reward for pressing a lever. When Skinner became a faculty member at the University of Minnesota, this work was expanded to pigeons.

Although Thorndike is often credited with being the first to outline operant conditioning concepts in his 1911 work *Animal Intelligence,* Skinner was the first to widely publicize this new technology. In 1938 Skinner published his findings in his book *The Behavior of Organisms*—a landmark work that was the first to fully define operant conditioning. With its publication, the science of operant conditioning was born. Skinner eventually joined the psychology faculty at Harvard University, where he wrote numerous books and papers and created the foundation for applying behavioral principles to humans and animals outside the laboratory setting.

In recent years, many dog trainers have attended seminars where they have learned to use a clicker. Clickers are *conditioned reinforcers,* as described by Skinner. Many trainers, filled with excitement, have told us about this "new" training method that was "invented by" the person conducting the seminar they attended. In fact, clicker training was being used by operant conditioning experts in the 1940s. In 1951, Skinner described the use of the clicker (which he called a *cricket*) in his paper *How to Teach Animals.*

A **conditioner reinforcer** depends on some conditioning taking place. In other words, you have to associate it with something pleasant before it will reinforce a behavior.

Partly because of Skinner's efforts to move beyond the lab, operant conditioning started as a science, but it has expanded to become both a science and a technology for changing behavior. In addition to widespread applications in dog training, Skinner's early operant conditioning work in the lab underwent a dramatic evolution and ultimately had a major impact in education, rehabilitation, business and industry.

THE FIRST TEXTBOOK

Fred S. Keller (1899–1996) was a classmate and lifelong friend of Skinner. Although Skinner taught at Harvard and Keller at Columbia, they were colleagues throughout their lives. Keller is well known for his work on a teaching method known as Personalized System of Instruction, or PSI. This is an individually paced, mastery-oriented way of teaching. Keller's visionary work in the late 1950s and early 1960s had many of the same components as today's computer-delivered instructional programs.

In 1947 at Columbia, Keller and William Schoenfeld began teaching the first college psychology course to use Skinner's methods. For the first time, undergraduate psychology students taught rats to respond to stimuli to obtain reinforcement. In 1950, Keller and Schoenfeld published their textbook *Principles of Psychology*. This was the first text for the exciting new field of operant conditioning.

APPLIED BEHAVIOR ANALYSIS

Researchers in the 1950s and 1960s got busy evaluating how operant conditioning could be used outside of the lab with humans. Using Skinner's model, they studied the behavior of children in schools, children in institutions, adults in a variety of settings and patients in mental institutions.

Most of the operant conditioning studies done with humans in the early 1950s were demonstrations that were not practical and did not result in a person acquiring functional skills or having a better life. But in 1959, Jack Michael and one of his doctoral students, Ted Allyon, changed that. Working at a psychiatric institution in Canada, Allyon and Michael trained institution staff to use operant conditioning procedures to modify patient behaviors such as refusing to eat, being aggressive and disruptive, and engaging in delusional talk. When this important work was published, the power and potential of operant conditioning to change people's lives became clear.

Applied behavior analysis is the term used when behavioral procedures are applied in real-world, nonlaboratory settings to improve the life of a human or animal.

In 1982, Michael coined the term *establishing operations*. These are events that affect the value of a stimulus to act as a reinforcer. (You'll find more information about establishing operations in Chapter 3 and Chapter 17.) In other words, the effectiveness of a reinforcer may be different at a particular time or in a particular situation.

In dog training, understanding the idea of establishing operations can often shed light on a dog's behavior. For example, a dog that is accustomed to eating at a certain time may engage in some unusual behaviors when dinner is late. A normally well-behaved dog might start rummaging in the garbage for food, licking crumbs off the kitchen floor or sneaking food from its owner's plate. For this dog, in this circumstance, food deprivation has

GETTING ORGANIZED

Following the publication of Michael and Allyon's first applied behavior analysis study, scientific journals and professional organizations were founded to encourage professional development and to support research. In 1958, the Society for the Experimental Analysis of Behavior (SEAB) was organized. SEAB introduced the *Journal of the Experimental Analysis of Behavior* (JEAB). JEAB is devoted to basic (rather than applied) animal and human research.

In 1968, to meet the needs of applied researchers, SEAB began publishing the *Journal of Applied Behavior Analysis* (JABA). Basic and applied researchers formed the Association for Behavior Analysis (ABA) in 1974 in order to promote the experimental analysis of behavior in applied settings. ABA provided applied researchers with their own organization, conferences and professional network.

In May 1994 at the annual ABA conference, animal trainers from across the country came together to form the ABA Animal Trainer's Forum, a special interest group of ABA. These are trainers who want to study the science of animal training. Members of the forum produce a newsletter, give presentations at the annual ABA conference, and work on projects related to animal training throughout the year. This group became the first professional forum to give large numbers of animal trainers and scientists the opportunity to participate in the same professional organization, thus furthering the understanding of the science behind animal training.

become an establishing operation. Food has become a powerful enough reward that the dog is willing to throw that advanced obedience title out the window and break the house rules.

ANIMAL TRAINING LEAVES THE LAB

In 1938, Marian Kruse was B.F. Skinner's research assistant. Among other duties, she trained the rats he worked with. In a twist of fate, one day she was bitten by a rat. On her way to get treatment, she met Keller Breland, an ambitious graduate student in psychology. They were married in 1941, just as the United States was going to war.

Skinner thought the new science of operant conditioning could be used to help the war efforts. With the Brelands as trainers, Project Pelican was started. Project Pelican trained pigeons to guide bombs that the Navy called *pelicans*. By 1942, equipment had been designed that made use of operant conditioning procedures to teach pigeons to guide a projectile by pecking when a military target was displayed.

Marian Breland Bailey and Keller Breland taught an astonishing array of tricks to thousands of animals.

When Project Pelican ended in 1943, Marion Breland went on to train animals for commercials and animal shows. Her trained chickens were used to advertise farm feeds. By 1947, Animal Behavior Enterprises, the Brelands' company, had set up thousands of animal shows nationwide. These animal shows were often seen in malls, fairs or arcades. Ducks and chickens were placed in Skinner boxes, which are cages with a Plexiglas front. Through operant conditioning, they learned how to turn on lights, play baseball, dance, play small pianos and do other tricks in order to receive food when a key was pecked. More sophisticated acts for television included cows, rabbits and pigs. One pig entertained audiences with scent discrimination exercises and by vacuuming, going on a simulated shopping trip and other behaviors.

The work of Keller Breland, Marion Breland Bailey and Bob Bailey was the first commercial application of the science of operant conditioning.

In 1951, Marion and Keller Breland published a paper titled *Applied Animal Psychology* that described how operant conditioning can be used to teach animals. Their work went mainstream in the 1950s with stories in *Time, Life* and *The Wall Street Journal*. Miami's Parrot Jungle hired the Brelands to develop parrot acts. Marine Studios in Florida also worked with them. Their work developing a dolphin act for Marine Studios resulted in the publication of the first manual for dolphin trainers.

When the Brelands got involved with dolphins, Bob Bailey, a zoologist from the University of California at Los Angeles and the Navy's Director of Training, entered the picture. Bailey worked with the Brelands to establish the Dolphins at Sea program for the Navy. Military work with animals continued over the years, and in 1965 Bailey developed an ambush detection system for the Army that involved using operant conditioning to teach pigeons.

Keller Breland died in 1965. Marion Breland and Bob Bailey continued the work of Animal Behavior Enterprises and were married in 1976. Over the years, the Baileys trained more than 140 species of birds and mammals by applying the sound scientific principles of operant conditioning. Bob Bailey is known for his work in using a *bridging stimulus*, a method of using a time bridge between the animal's response and the delivery of a primary reinforcer such as food.

Primary reinforcers are those reinforcers that are related to biological drives, such as food and sex.

Along with Skinner, Keller Breland and the Baileys were the true pioneers of many of the animal training practices we see today, including the use of conditioned reinforcers such as clickers.

Bob Bailey worked with dolphins on U.S. Navy projects. Conditioned reinforcement is used to train dolphins.

Chapter 2

the trainers

···

How dog training evolved to embrace
operant conditioning

The first dog owners to observe how dogs learn were no doubt the cave-men who brought wolf cubs into their dens to serve as companions. Primitive drawings in cave dwellings show that the importance of animals in our lives began with our earliest human ancestors.

Dogs have been trained for centuries to help humans. Some time between 127 and 116 B.C., a Roman farmer named Marcus Varro recorded tips on training and raising puppies to be used for herding. In 55 B.C., Roman armies marched into the British countryside accompanied by their drover's dogs. These dogs either followed commands or were left behind, so natural selection took care of the ones that did not respond to training.

In the year 943, a Welsh king wrote about herding dogs that could take sheep to the field during the day and return them home at night.

Even though instinct played a large role in the ability of these early working dogs, there is no doubt that they had some training. Farmers, hunters and shepherds who depended on flocks and herds for their liveli-hood most likely became dog trainers simply because they had to.

SPORTING DOGS

As the dog world got a bit more organized, so did dog training. Early dog shows in Britain in the 1700s and 1800s focused on exhibiting the dogs, but the dogs most often exhibited were sporting breeds that were well trained.

As in Britain, the earliest interest in organized dog training in the United States focused on sporting dogs. In the 1700s, George Washington maintained a kennel of Foxhounds at Mount Vernon, and competitions involving pointers, setters and hounds were popular.

The idea of training a dog simply to be a better companion took a long time to catch on, especially in the United States. By the 1920s there were boarding kennels where owners could send their dogs off to be trained by professionals, but very few people cared much about training.

TRAINING TO COMPETE

Training dogs for competition and to earn obedience titles didn't begin in this country until 1933, when Helene Whitehouse Walker decided to show everyone that her dog was far more than just another pretty face. Walker was a breeder of Standard Poodles —dogs that were thought of by many at the time as sissies. She knew about the behavior tests that were being held in England for working dogs, and had an idea for something similar in the United States.

An effective and persuasive woman, Walker began approaching dog clubs and breeders with her idea of holding competitive obedience tests at dog shows. In 1933 in Mount Kisco, New York, eight dogs competed in America's first obedience trial. The slogan "Train Your Dog" became popular across the country, and in 1934 the North Westchester Kennel Club and Somerset Hills Kennel Club held obedience tests at their dog shows. By 1936, the American Kennel Club had developed and was using the *Regulations and Standards for Obedience Test Trials* at licensed obedience events.

Inspired by the public's enthusiastic response to obedience and dog training, in 1937 Walker, her friend Blanche Saunders, and their dogs went on the road in a 21-foot trailer to give obedience demonstrations across the country. In 1941, the New England Dog Training Club became the first obedience club to become a member of the AKC. Dog training had arrived.

THE MOST FAMOUS CAVALRY SOLDIER

From the 1920s to the 1950s, Americans of all ages watched with wonder as a German Shepherd entertained and amazed them. The dog belonged to Lee Duncan, a World War I soldier who found a shell-shocked puppy in the French trenches. He took the dog home, and in 1922 Rin Tin Tin made his movie debut.

Rin Tin Tin was so popular that he was credited with saving the Warner Brothers movie studio from bankruptcy in the 1920s. Referred to as "the

U.S. Cavalry's most valuable soldier," Rin Tin Tin would make spectacular leaps over raging river rapids, hide under the water from a pursuer, and hold the reins in his mouth to drive a horse and buggy.

Rin Tin Tin died at the age of 16 and was buried in Paris. At the time of his death, he was receiving 2,000 fan letters every week, showing that people of all ages and backgrounds were fascinated with the idea of a highly trained dog.

THE TRADITION OF LASSIE

A 1938 story involving a Collie started a tradition that lasted more than 50 years. The story was about Joe, a boy whose family had to sell their Collie because they could not afford to keep it. The story touched the hearts of so many people that it was eventually made into a novel and a movie starring Elizabeth Taylor and Roddy McDowall. Pal, the original Lassie, made his debut in that 1943 film, *Lassie Come Home.*

The movie was so popular that it was made into a television series. For many people growing up in the 1950s, Sunday nights were the high point of the week. It was then that we could watch a beautiful, well-trained dog who was so devoted she would travel for miles and would overcome any obstacles to get to her owner. It was the human-animal bond at its finest.

Rudd Weatherwax was Pal's trainer, and eight generations of Lassies later, Rudd's son Bob is carrying on the tradition of training Lassies using positive training methods.

THE FIRST CURRICULUM

While Pavlov was studying reflexive responses in dogs and Walker was criss-crossing the United States in a trailer to promote obedience training, in Germany, Colonel Conrad Most was training dogs and explaining their learning tendencies from a dog trainer's perspective. Most started training police dogs in 1906, and by the 1940s he was using his knowledge to teach the handlers and trainers of dogs at the German Dog Farm, a training center for guide dogs and their blind handlers.

Most demonstrated an understanding of operant conditioning concepts such as primary and secondary reinforcement, shaping, fading and chaining 28 years before the publication of B.F. Skinner's *The Behavior of Organisms.* He differentiated between primary and secondary reinforcers, and referred to secondary reinforcers as *secondary inducements.* He used his voice and soft tones as secondary inducements, much the way some trainers use clickers today.

Operant Conditioning:
A Basic Timeline

Year	Scientists/Researchers	Dog Trainers
1800s	• Pavlov (1849–1936) • Respondent conditioning • Conditioned reflexes	• American Kennel Club formed (1884)
1900–1920s	• E.L. Thorndike's Law of Effect (1911) • J.B. Watson's Stimulus-Response psychology (1913–1924)	• Dog training becoming more popular in the U.S., but no formal training events • Col. Conrad Most in Germany writes *Training Dogs*, one of the first "how to" manuals Describes principles similar to Skinner's (1910)
1930s	• B.F. Skinner's Behavior of Organisms (1938)	• Helene Whitehouse Walker organizes first obedience trial (1933) • Obedience trials at conformation shows (1934) • AKC obedience regulations in place (1936) • Walker and Blanche Saunders cross the country giving obedience demonstrations
1940s	• Project Pelican–Skinner and the Brelands (1942) • Animal Behavior Enterprises–animal shows and training • First undergrad college course in operant conditioning taught by Keller and Schoenfeld (1947)	• New England Dog Training Club is the first obedience/training club to become a member club of the AKC (1941)
1950s	• Skinner describes teaching animals with clickers (1951) • Brelands publish a paper on applied animal psychology and training • First undergrad college text for operant conditioning by Keller Schoenfeld (1950) • Allyon & Michael bring operant conditioning out of the lab with applied behavior analysis (1959)	• Bill Koehler's movie dogs Wildfire and the Shaggy Dog • Lassie and Rin Tin Tin on television • Saunders' *Complete Book of Dog Training* (1954) • Milo Pearsall's *Dog Obedience Training* shows some awareness of Pavlov (1958)

Year	Scientists/Researchers	Dog Trainers
1960s	• Bob Bailey uses operant conditioning with military animals (1965) • *Journal of Applied Behavior Analysis* (1968)	• *Koehler Method of Dog Training* (1962) • Clarence Pfaffenberger's *New Knowledge of Dog Behavior* (1963) • Winifred Strickland's *Expert Obedience Training for Dogs* (1965) • Scott & Fuller's *Dog Behavior: The Genetic Basis* (1965)
1970s	• Association for Behavior Analysis formed (1974)	• Bill Campbell's *Behavior Problems in Dogs* (1975) • *Front & Finish* dog training magazine started by Bob Self; includes behavioral articles • *Off-Lead* dog training magazine started by Don Arner; includes behavioral articles
1980s	• Language of operant conditioning continues to be clarified. Establishing operations described by Jack Michael (1982) • Karen Pryor gives the keynote address to the Association for Behavior Analysis and describes to scientists the potential use of operant conditioning with dog trainers.	• Ian Dunbar offers seminars, books and videos promoting the use of food lures and rewards • Karen Pryor's seminars for dog trainers teach principles of operant conditioning • Karen Pryor's *Don't Shoot the Dog* takes operant conditioning to the public (1984)
1990s	• Association for Behavior Analysis (ABA) Trainers Forum forms, including both dog trainers and scientists (1994)	• Several trainers offer clicker training seminars and have written materials and videos • Dog trainers join ABA (1994) • Association of Pet Dog Trainers (APDT) forms (1994) • APDT conference program including a variety of operant conditioning topics (1997) • Too many curriculums, videos, etc. for training dogs to list

Like many trainers who came from a police or military background, Most used procedures that would be regarded as heavy-handed by today's trainers. Nonetheless, it is important to recognize that an early dog trainer had independently discovered many of the relationships between consequences and behavior that Skinner would later describe. Most's 1910 manual *Training Dogs* was one of the first "how-to" dog training books.

> Most described reinforcement as "that agreeable experience when the dog has performed a correct behavior."

WILLIAM KOEHLER

Like Conrad Most, Bill Koehler began by training military dogs. But after World War II, Koehler became chief trainer for the Orange Empire Dog Club. This club was known for its consistently winning performances in team obedience competitions, and for the large numbers of obedience titles its members racked up. Koehler and his son Dick also trained students at their own training facility. By 1960, more than 40,000 dogs were trained in classes at Koehler's school.

Koehler is credited with starting the use of long lines and light lines in training—methods designed to improve attentiveness and off-leash control. As the head animal trainer for Walt Disney Studios, he introduced millions of Americans to the potential of obedience training when Wildfire, a Bull Terrier, was named Outstanding Animal Actor of 1955 for his role in *It's a Dog's Life*.

The Koehler method of training is based largely on the principles of negative reinforcement and punishment. The idea of negative reinforcement is that the dog does what you want him to do in order to escape an unpleasant experience.

One of the most frequently used examples of negative reinforcement in dog training is the use of the choke chain, also known as a training collar. After experiencing unpleasant jerks on the chain, many dogs work hard to avoid the jerk. Koehler used choke chains as part of procedures such as turning quickly and going in the opposite direction when the dog was forging ahead or pulling the handler.

> In operant conditioning, *negative reinforcement* means removing an unpleasant event as soon as a desired response has been performed, in order to increase the frequency of the response.

An example of punishment in the Koehler method is the use of throw chains. Koehler used throw chains to control the dog from a distance. For example, if the dog was called and did not respond, the chain would be thrown sharply at the dog's rear. According to Koehler, as the chain hits the dog, the handler should reel in the leash and have the dog sit in front. When the dog is positioned in front, Koehler said handlers should provide lavish praise, showing that he believes in positively reinforcing dogs for what they have done correctly.

In training, Koehler advocated letting dogs make mistakes, having those mistakes generate consequences and then providing praise for desired behavior. In cases where dogs had behavior problems such as digging, jumping on people or barking, Koehler believed in the use of punishment. For dogs that were diggers, Koehler advised digging a hole, filling it with water and putting the dog's nose into the water. According to the Koehler methods, dogs that jump on people should receive a sharp knee in the chest, and dogs that bark excessively should be hit with a leather belt.

Times have changed since Koehler started training dogs. While he stood by his techniques throughout his life, Koehler's punishment procedures are not considered necessary, humane or appropriate by many of today's trainers. The paradigm shift in dog training seems to match changes that have occurred over the years in treating people with disabilities and mental health problems. In the 1960s, patients in institutions were treated with shock therapy, and aversive stimuli such as lemon juice and ammonia were routinely used with patients who had behavior problems. It was believed then that punishment was the fastest, most effective way to fix a severe behavior problem.

Punishment, in the operant conditioning context, is defined as providing a consequence that makes a particular behavior less likely to occur in the future.

With the exception of a few unusual cases in highly specialized treatment facilities, these procedures are not used today and would be considered abusive. Like human therapies, for the most part dog training has undergone an evolution and moved toward a more positive approach.

We met Bill Koehler and watched him work with dogs and students in the 1980s. He appeared then to be a kind and gentle man, and he clearly loved dogs. At the time Koehler developed his procedures, he was one of the few people in the country who was known for his ability to rehabilitate tough dogs. For many dogs, Koehler was their last hope.

While the trend in the 1980s and 1990s has been toward positive approaches to dog training, and many of Koehler's procedures are criticized, Bill Koehler cannot be denied recognition for the major impact he had on dog training in this country.

BLANCHE SAUNDERS

After Blanche Saunders' and Helene Whitehouse Walker's incredible cross-country journey to sell the benefits of dog training to the American public, Saunders continued to promote the newly emerging sport of obedience with missionary zeal. She organized obedience demonstrations at high-visibility events, such as the Westminster Dog Show held in Rockefeller Center during National Dog Week, and at ballgames in Yankee Stadium with 70,000 spectators.

In 1954, Saunders published *The Complete Book of Dog Obedience*. This was the first book written specifically for obedience instructors, and in it Saunders outlined the format for procedures that would be adopted in dog training classes across the country.

Saunders said, "Dogs learn by associating their act with a pleasing or displeasing result. They must be disciplined when they do wrong, but they must also be rewarded when they do right." She advocated the use of punishment for some behavior problems.

Negative reinforcement played a key part in Saunders' method. Perhaps the most frequently used negative reinforcer is the jerking of the choke chain. When a dog receives a jerk from the choke collar, the procedure is technically considered punishment. However, when the dog hears the zipper sound of the collar as the trainer prepares for a correction and works to avoid the correction, the procedure is negative reinforcement.

In the Saunders method, to teach heeling, students are instructed to learn the sequence, "Heel! Jerk! Praise!" Jerks are also used to teach behaviors such as sit and down, and to correct problems such as inattentiveness.

Food training was virtually unknown when Saunders was training dogs, and she specifically stated that trainers should never use food in training. Saunders primarily used pats and praise as reinforcers. To teach new skills, she often used physical prompts. Dogs were taught to lie down by having the handler step on the shortened leash. In teaching dogs to sit, handlers would apply pressure to the dog's shoulder to guide it into position. She believed food should not be given "like a bribe" on an ongoing basis, but that it was acceptable to use "a tidbit now and then to overcome a problem." This was perhaps the beginning of the shift away from military and police training methods that relied primarily on punishment, escape and avoidance behaviors.

Throughout *The Complete Book of Dog Obedience*, Saunders advocated praise, kindness and fairness. She listed "too little praise" as one of the most common mistakes of dog owners. Saunders was perhaps the first author to repeatedly stress the importance of reinforcement in training, thus starting the trend toward the positive training methods used today.

MILO PEARSALL

Milo Pearsall's 1958 book *Dog Obedience Training* has been billed as the book that revolutionized dog training with a more gentle approach. However, many of Pearsall's training methods were the same negative reinforcement techniques described four years earlier by Blanche Saunders. A snap on the leash was his preferred correction in teaching the dog to heel, to sit and to improve attentiveness.

Pearsall also used punishment to correct problem behaviors. To correct dogs that jump on people, Pearsall suggested the person knee the dog in the chest. To stop car chasing, owners were told to tie a stick to a short length of rope hanging from the dog's collar. As the dog ran to chase, the stick hit against the dog's front legs. For housebreaking accidents, Pearsall suggested that owners push their dog's noses near the accident (not in it) so that the dog could get the idea of what it had done wrong (something we now know has absolutely no corrective effect on house soiling). In the Pearsall method, dogs that ran away were trained on a long line. When they tried to bolt with the long line attached to their collar, they were jerked off their feet.

In 1958, Pearsall wrote, "The dog at first learns his lessons by the application of a primary stimulus—forcing him to sit, for example—and at the same time a secondary stimulus, the command, is given to him. Soon, the secondary means exactly the same to him as the primary did. The best-known example of this primary-secondary transfer is the famous experiment of Pavlov on the salivation of dogs."

Unfortunately, while Pearsall knew that there was a connection between learning theory and dog training, he confused the concepts of reflex conditioning (as in Pavlov's work) with operant conditioning, which reflects learning. A dog learning to sit when the physical prompt of forcing him into a sit has been paired with the verbal cue "sit" is clearly an example of operant conditioning.

Dogs are amazing creatures, and they often learn despite the confusing messages we send them. For serious infractions, Pearsall said the dog should be struck under the chin with the fingers. As soon as the dog was hit for misbehavior, he instructed the handler to immediately praise the dog.

Behaviorally, we now know it would not make sense to give a reinforcer immediately after a punisher. Such a pairing would clearly cause the punisher to take on reinforcing qualities. According to sound behavioral principles, the reinforcer (praise) should not be given until the dog engages in an acceptable behavior. Then, that behavior should be reinforced.

Pearsall justified the practice of praise as soon as you punish by saying the handler needed to "let the dog know he was still loved" and that the handler was on the dog's side. It's hard to say exactly what the handler was really communicating to the dog, but many dogs still managed to learn what was considered correct behavior and what was not.

In operant conditioning, the word *punishment* is a technical term that means "to provide a consequence that makes a particular behavior less likely to occur in the future." For example, if you grabbed the handle of a pan you were cooking with and were severely burned, in operant conditioning terms you were punished for grabbing the handle of the pan while cooking. But Pearsall, like many trainers, did not use the operant conditioning definition of punishment. He equated punishment with a crime, retribution or a person just trying to get even. Using that definition, he was correct in stating that a dog "does not, and never will, understand punishment."

WINIFRED STRICKLAND

Winifred Strickland began competing in obedience in the 1940s and became one of the first super trainers, earning 160 titles and 40 perfect scores. In Strickland's 1965 book *Expert Obedience Training for Dogs*, she outlined a method that promoted a kinder, more humane method of training.

Strickland did not use food to train, saying that food "will only work with dogs that think more of their own stomachs than their owners." Her comment, "Do not be embarassed if someone overhears you praising your dog. Be proud of it," shows us just how far training has come in the last 30 years.

THE DOG BEHAVIOR CLASSICS

In the years before the term operant conditioning was familiar to dog trainers, well-known trainers introduced new methods or modifications of old ones with a steady regularity. However, despite a consistently growing number of books and seminars on how to train, leading trainers have understood for decades that more is required to train a dog than a set of procedures or a bag of tricks.

Good trainers understand the whole dog. Although we can make some generalizations about learning theory and what happens when an animal is reinforced or punished, we cannot deny the roles that genetics and breed or species differences play when we are trying to change an animal's behavior. Several classic works have served as guides in helping trainers understand the big picture when working with dogs.

Clarence Pfaffenberger

In 1963, Clarence Pfaffenberger published *The New Knowledge of Dog Behavior.* Pfaffenberger was known for his work with Guide Dogs for the Blind and Dogs for Defense—a wartime program in which donated dogs were screened for potential military use and provided with training if accepted.

In both programs, Pfaffenberger was responsible for screening dogs. He developed some of the earliest behavior and temperament assessments, and described how important a knowledge of genetics is in breeding dogs to perform specific tasks.

Scott and Fuller

Drs. John Paul Scott and John Fuller published *Dog Behavior: The Genetic Basis* in 1965. This work, published later as *Genetics and the Social Behavior of the Dog*, is considered by many to be the most comprehensive study of dog behavior ever published. Scott and Fuller spent more than 20 years as canine researchers at the Roscoe B. Jackson Laboratory in Bar Harbor, Maine. Their work emphasizes the critical role that heredity plays in the development of canine behavior. Scott was also one of the founding members of the Animal Behavior Society.

In *Genetics and the Social Behavior of the Dog*, Scott and Fuller refer to the operant conditioning work of B.F. Skinner as well as the work of Keller and Marian Breland. Scott and Fuller are well known for identifying the critical socialization periods for puppies. Their research, showing that breeds have significant differences when it comes to emotional and motivational characteristics, is of tremendous importance to dog owners who wish to understand the whole dog.

Pfaffenberger worked closely with Scott and Fuller. In fact, Scott has given Pfaffenberger credit for testing many of his laboratory-generated theories about dogs in real-life settings.

William Campbell

William Campbell's *Behavior Problems in Dogs* has been a reference work for animal behaviorists, veterinarians and trainers since the first edition of the book was published in 1975. *Behavior Problems in Dogs* was based on Campbell's experience in consulting on thousands of cases. Well-versed in

---

MAGAZINES FOR DOG TRAINERS

There are two magazines written exclusively for dog trainers, and in recent years both have seen an increase in articles about operant conditioning, or the science of how dogs learn.

Front & Finish

Front & Finish is a monthly magazine that dog trainers have been reading for over 20 years. Started by Bob Self and currently managed by Robert Self, Jr., this newspaper-format publication features articles on formal obedience competition and general dog training issues. In addition, *Front & Finish* devotes a great deal of space to publicizing the accomplishments of dog trainers.

Bob Self was an AKC obedience judge who was well known for the obedience seminars he conducted with Jack Godsil. For many years, Godsil was one of the country's leading obedience exhibitors, and Bob Self was his mentor.

Off-Lead

Started more than 20 years ago by Lorenz Arner, the monthly magazine *Off-Lead* is currently managed by Mark Arner. Articles are written for dog trainers, and include instruction on how to run training classes as well as general dog training issues.

---

operant conditioning procedures, Campbell provides solutions to the whole range of problem behaviors dogs may exhibit.

His solutions go beyond using operant procedures and include considerations such as family dynamics, the dog's medical condition, problems associated with aging, environmental modifications and nutrition. Campbell currently publishes the *Pet Behavior Newsletter* four times a year. This newsletter features many case studies that involve using operant conditioning to treat behavior problems, as well as a variety of informational articles pertinent to dog behavior.

Ian Dunbar

Dr. Ian Dunbar is a veterinarian and animal behaviorist. In the 1980s Dunbar was teaching seminars in which he explained operant terminology and how specific behavioral concepts related to dog behavior problems. Dunbar recognized that most people do not like to use aversive corrections with their dogs, and he developed a positive, motivational training method using food rewards that unskilled trainers could learn to use effectively.

In 1994, Dunbar played a key role in founding the Association of Pet Dog Trainers (APDT). By 1997, the conference program included a number of topics related to operant conditioning such as punishment, how to use and time reinforcers, and stimulus control. In the last 20 years many trainers have shared Dunbar's desire that dog training become more positive in nature. Dunbar, however, has been unique in that he has demonstrated a remarkable ability to promote the concept on a very large scale.

Karen Pryor

Karen Pryor is a scientist, writer, animal trainer and seminar leader. For dog trainers in the 1980s and 1990s, Pryor also fulfilled an important role as a translator of basic behavioral concepts for animal trainers. Pryor began working with marine mammals, using Skinner's operant conditioning principles to teach dolphins and develop marine mammal shows. In 1984, she published her book *Don't Shoot the Dog*, an explanation of operant procedures written for the general public. In it, Pryor used real-world situations to demonstrate how operant conditioning can be used to change the behavior of one's children, spouse, roommate or pets.

Karen Pryor introduced operant conditioning principles to the general public.

When *Reader's Digest* published an excerpt of *Don't Shoot the Dog,* many behaviorists were ecstatic that someone had successfully introduced operant conditioning to the general public. In the late 1980s, Pryor gave the keynote address to behavioral scientists at the Association for Behavior Analysis international conference, and the bridge between science and modern day dog training was built.

Pryor's training materials and seminars showed how operant procedures can be used to provide training that is positive. Pryor also introduced trainers to concepts such as secondary reinforcement with her shaping game and examples of clicker training.

By the mid-1990s, there were several dog trainers writing and conducting national seminars on how to use clickers in training. Numerous dog trainers were giving workshops and writing on operant conditioning topics such as positive reinforcement, shaping behaviors and decreasing undesirable behaviors. The long-term impact of these trainers on the field of dog training is not yet known. What is known is that by the 1990s, due to Pryor's earlier work, the dog training world knew about operant conditioning.

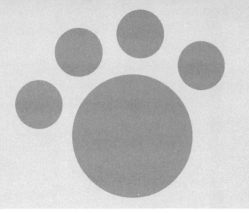

Part Two

the basic principles of behavior

To understand how operant conditioning works, we must first understand some basic principles of behavior. The principles of reinforcement, extinction, punishment and stimulus control can be used to explain the behavior of animals or people.

Chapter 3

reinforcement

....

What dogs like, what they want to avoid, what they'll work for

Understanding reinforcement is the key to understanding how learning takes place. From a behaviorist's perspective, each day is made up of a series of behaviors that are either reinforced or not reinforced. This is true for both animals and humans. The reinforcement that occurs, along with the strength and timing of that reinforcement, will determine whether the behaviors are likely to occur again.

> **Reinforcement** occurs when a behavior, followed by a consequent stimulus, is strengthened, or becomes more likely to occur again.

A *stimulus* is any object or event that can be detected by the senses and that can affect a person's or an animal's behavior.

Stimuli (the plural of stimulus) can be sounds, food or drinks, smells, touches or visual signals.

In dog training, trainers are said to be providing reinforcement when they provide consequences that increase or maintain a behavior. Some examples of stimuli that affect behavior in dogs include verbal commands, encouraging noises, clickers or whistles, food treats, pats or snaps on a leash.

In operant conditioning, reinforcement can be categorized as either primary or secondary, or as either positive or negative. Let's take a look at what these variables really mean.

PRIMARY REINFORCEMENT: WILL WORK FOR FOOD

Primary reinforcers are reinforcers that are related to biology. Examples of primary reinforcers include food, drink, some kinds of touch and sexual contact.

When dogs are trained using treats, that is a primary reinforcer.

But primary reinforcers are more than food. For some breeds that are innately wired to be visual, visual stimuli seem to be primary reinforcers. Because of selective breeding over many centuries,

A **reinforcer** is a stimulus that, when presented following a behavior, causes that behavior to be more likely to occur again in the future.

many sporting dogs are very visually oriented. Some spaniels will look out a window and notice a leaf falling from a tree across the street. Owners of dogs with such finely tuned sensitivities often wonder why their dog isn't paying attention in an outdoor obedience class. "I'm giving him treats," they tell us, not understanding that for this dog, a treat just can't compete with the field full of birds across the road.

SECONDARY REINFORCEMENT: "GOOD BOY!"

Secondary reinforcers are reinforcers that can be related to social conditions. In other words, they have a cultural context. Humans respond to secondary reinforcers such as praise, smiles, thumbs-up gestures and money. Dogs are social creatures, and many dogs also respond well to smiles, praise, attention, clapping, toys and pats. But, just as we have to learn that thumbs-up means

"well done," dogs have to learn that praise is something positive.

Verbal praise is the most commonly used secondary reinforcer. When a dog is a young puppy, saying "good girl" to her has no meaning. It's just a bunch of

Secondary reinforcers become reinforcing by being paired with primary reinforcers.

sounds. But when you say "good girl" and give her a piece of food or a pat, she learns to associate praise with good things. Praise has become a secondary reinforcer.

Secondary reinforcers are also called *conditioned reinforcers*. This is because secondary reinforcers depend upon some conditioning taking place. For example, if a dog owner takes the leash out of a particular drawer just before taking her dog for a walk, taking the leash out of the drawer can become a conditioned reinforcer. If one day the dog is chewing on a shoe when she takes out the leash, chewing on a shoe may accidentally become reinforced; the dog may think that going for a walk is its reward for chewing on the shoe.

A **conditioned reinforcer** is a previously neutral stimulus that begins to function as a reinforcer after being paired a number of times with an established reinforcer.

In place of verbal praise, some trainers use sounds as conditioned reinforcers that essentially mean "good job!" In marine mammal shows at places like Sea World, when the porpoise trainers blow a whistle to let the animal know it has performed correctly, the trainers are delivering conditioned reinforcement. Conditioned reinforcement is a way a trainer can offer reinforcement from a distance and when it is not handy to give food to the animal. Applause is another conditioned reinforcer, for both human performers and many competition dogs.

Now We're Clicking

Recently, the dog training community has seen an increase in the use of clicker training, which uses the clicker as a conditioned reinforcer. The clicker is a small metal and plastic device that makes a clicking sound. Clickers have been around for decades. Years ago they were called "crickets" and were sold as children's toys.

When clickers are used as conditioned reinforcers, the dog is first given food alone as a primary reinforcer. Once the dog has clearly shown that it likes food, the pairing begins. The clicker is clicked; then the food is given. Because the clicking sound is associated with the delivery of food, the click alone begins to take on reinforcing properties. (You'll find more information about clicker training in Chapter 14.)

Clicker training is one application of conditioned reinforcement. The clicker is a neutral stimulus that is followed by a primary reinforcer, and eventually becomes a conditioned reinforcer.

The clicker is a conditioned reinforcer because it started out as a neutral stimulus, meaning it had no meaning for the dog. But when it was paired with food, the dog eventually learned that a clicker also means "good job!"

How Reinforcement Becomes Conditioned

Symbols for Explaining Conditioning

S^D = The cue, "fetch the paper"

R = The response, fetching the paper

S^N = The neutral stimulus, "good dog"

S^{R+} = The primary reinforcer, dog biscuits

Step 1. $S^D \rightarrow R \rightarrow S^N \rightarrow S^{R+}$

In the presence of the **cue** ("fetch the paper") Laddie emits the **response** (fetching the paper) and is immediately given the **neutral stimulus** ("good dog"), which is then followed by the **primary reinforcer** (dog biscuits). This is done several times.

Step 2. $S^D \rightarrow R \rightarrow S^{R+}$

The neutral stimulus, after several repetitions, becomes a **conditioned reinforcer** (S^R+) capable of acting as a primary reinforcer.

Step 3. For the conditioned reinforcer to **maintain** its effectiveness, it should be followed occasionally (such as every third to tenth time) by the primary reinforcer, food.

POSITIVE REINFORCEMENT: WILL STILL WORK FOR FOOD

Reinforcement can also be described as positive or negative: something an animal wants to acquire more of, or something it wants to escape from or avoid.

A **positive reinforcer** is a stimulus that, when presented following a behavior, makes it more likely that type of behavior will occur in the future.

The delivery of a positive reinforcer results in positive reinforcement. Here are some examples of positive reinforcement.

Sugar was an English Cocker Spaniel being trained for obedience. In obedience competition, dogs are expected to sit straight in front of their owners, at a precise 90-degree angle, and are penalized for crooked sits. Sugar was sitting straight only some of the time in obedience routines. During training, Sugar's owner began giving her a small piece of dog food when she sat straight, and no food when she sat crooked. Within a few sessions, Sugar was sitting straight.

Dog Situation →	Dog Behavior →	Trainer Response →	Results (Consequences)
Sugar was a spaniel being trained for obedience	Sugar would come to her owner and sit crooked some of the time	Give treats for straight sits (food = primary, positive reinforcement)	Straight sits increased

Sam was a five-year-old Vizsla whose owner decide to take him to non-competitive field dog training classes as a leisure activity. Sam was initially more interested in his owner than in finding the birds. In training, as he began to move away from his owner's side in the correct direction, she would excitedly say, "Good boy, good boy Sam!" Sam began wagging his tail and moving forward to find the birds.

Dog Situation →	Dog Behavior →	Trainer Response →	Results (Consequences)
Sam was a Vizsla being trained for field work	Sam was more interested in his owner than in finding birds	Trainer would excitedly say, "Good boy, good Sam," when Sam moved away from her toward the hidden birds (Praise = secondary, positive reinforcement)	Sam began moving out to find the birds

Cody was a German Shepherd that worked full time as a drug detection dog. Some nights, Cody had to search cars in an airport parking lot. When he stayed on-task and completed his searches, his trainer gave him his toy—a knotted towel that could be used to play tug-of-war. Cody's trainer decided that they could complete their evening duties faster if the playtime was eliminated. Soon after, Cody's searching and on-task behavior decreased. Cody's trainer restored playtime as a reward for searching, and Cody's on-task behavior improved.

Dog Situation →	Dog Behavior →	Trainer Response →	Results (Consequences)
Cody was a German Shepherd involved in drug detection work	Cody's searching behavior decreased when playtime was eliminated	Trainer resumed playtime following searches (Play and toy = secondary, positive reinforcement)	Cody' s on-task behavior improved

The positive reinforcers in these three examples are food, praise and a toy. What makes these items positive reinforcers is the effect each had on the behavior of the dog. In each case, the desired behavior increased when the positive stimulus was presented following the behavior. Given treats, Sugar's sits improved. When Sam was praised, he began moving in the desired direction. If a toy was offered after searches, Cody stayed on-task and searched.

Positive reinforcement can be used to:

- Improve proficiency
- Teach new skills
- Maintain existing behavior

The important thing to remember about positive reinforcement is that it must seem positive to the dog. Some dogs couldn't care less about a trainer saying, "Good boy." Dogs that eat dinner at 6 p.m. and go to obedience class at 7 p.m. may not find treats particularly reinforcing in class. If a dog has free access to a particular toy, that toy may not be a positive reinforcer. If you deliver what you think is a reinforcer and it does not result in the desired behavior, it's possible that what you think is a reinforcer and what the dog thinks is a reinforcer are two different things.

NEGATIVE REINFORCEMENT: ESCAPE FEELS GOOD

Negative reinforcement can be a confusing concept. Many people equate it with punishment, but these two operant conditioning principles are very different. Very simply put, negative reinforcement is used to get the dog to do something more often. Punishment gets the dog to stop doing something.

Punishment decreases the probability that a behavior will occur again. That is, if a dog is punished for a behavior and the punisher is effective, the dog will be less likely to engage in the punished behavior in the future.

Negative reinforcement, like positive reinforcement, will increase the likelihood that a behavior will occur again. So what's the difference? With positive reinforcement, a positive stimulus is used, such as food, toys or petting. With negative reinforcement, a negative stimulus is removed, conditioning an escape response.

With *negative reinforcement*, the probability of a behavior occurring in the future is increased when the behavior is followed by the removal or avoidance of a negative stimulus.

For example, some dogs are trained to heel with a chain training collar. When the dog lags behind the handler, the handler gives a snap-release correction on the collar. If the dog feels or hears the handler starting to make the correction and hurries to get into the heel position to avoid the correction, negative reinforcement has taken place.

Reinforcement Categories
and Sample Stimuli

	Primary Reinforcers (Unconditioned Reinforcers)	Secondary Reinforcers (Conditioned Reinforcers)
Positive Reinforcement	Presentation of: • Food • Drink • Exercise • Smells • Petting	Presentation of: • Toys • Praise ("good dog") • Attention (petting)
Negative Reinforcement	Removal of: • Shock (shock collar) • Pain (ear pinch) • Other (heat, bright light)	Removal of: • "Bad dog" • "No!" • Threatening tone of voice • Threatening gesture (raised hand)

Like secondary reinforcement, negative reinforcement must be conditioned. In other words, the dog has to have been exposed to some punishment and understand it as a negative experience. In the case of the training collar, there must be at least one experience where the dog actually receives the jerk on the collar and finds it unpleasant. When the dog hurries into heel position to avoid the jerk, learning has taken place.

POSITIVE AND NEGATIVE: HOW CAN THAT BE?

Some stimuli in the environment are positive reinforcers for some people (and dogs), and negative reinforcers for others. Heavy metal music blaring from a boom box at the beach may be a positive reinforcer for some teenagers, while others of us may respond to the same music by leaving the beach. For those who find escape from the music a relief, it's a negative reinforcer.

Individual dogs of the same breed can be as different as two people: one who likes loud music and another who detests it. And different breeds of dogs react differently to different stimuli. In dog training, selecting an effective reinforcement strategy depends on both your knowledge of behavioral principles and a good understanding of the individual dog.

You can also make choices about using neutral stimuli as positive or negative reinforcers. Some stimuli that are traditionally thought of as positive reinforcers may be used as negative reinforcers in dog training. Clickers are most often used as positive conditioned reinforcers. Paired with a food treat, clickers give the dog the message that it has behaved correctly. In a less traditional approach, some trainers use clickers to warn the dog that it must stop what it is doing. As with the positive approach, the clicker must initially be paired with a negative experience to make it function as a negative reinforcer.

ESCAPE CONDITIONING: OK, I'LL SAY "UNCLE"

Negative reinforcement works by making use of escape conditioning and avoidance conditioning. In *escape conditioning,* a response is more likely to occur in the future if the negative stimulus is removed immediately after the response. Here's an example.

Star was a Labrador Retriever being trained to work as a service dog. As part of her training, she had to learn to hold a wooden dumbbell as the first step in learning how to retrieve. However, Star refused to take the dumbbell in her mouth. She'd clench her teeth shut and would not give in. Her trainer used a common procedure of holding the dumbbell up to her mouth and then pinching her ear. When Star opened her mouth to take the dumbbell, her ear was released and she was praised for taking it.

In escape conditioning, escape comes *after* the aversive event has occurred.

Dog Situation →	Dog Behavior →	Trainer Response →	Results (Consequences)
Star was a Labrador Retriever that had to learn to hold a dumbbell	Star clenched her teeth and refused to take the dumbbell in her mouth	Trainer held the dumbbell at her mouth and pinched her ear (pinch = negative reinforcement escape conditioning)	Star opened her mouth, took the dumbbell and was praised

AVOIDANCE CONDITIONING: A WARNING

In *avoidance conditioning,* if a behavior can prevent a negative stimulus from occurring, the behavior increases in frequency. In order for this to happen, the dog must know that the negative stimulus is coming and must know what it can do to avoid the negative stimulus. This requires conditioning.

An example is Buddy, a Basset Hound whose owner wanted to take him for short walks in the neighborhood. But Buddy was more interested in his surroundings than in walking, and would stop every few feet to sniff and smell. It made walks tedious. His owner responded by making a loud, nasal noise that sounded a bit like a sneeze every time Buddy stopped. The noise was always followed by a jerk on the leash. When Buddy started walking, he was praised. After several corrections, Buddy understood that the noise came just before a correction. And the praise taught him that he was supposed to be walking. So whenever he heard the noise, he kept walking in order to avoid the correction.

> In avoidance conditioning, avoidance occurs *before* the aversive event takes place.

Dog Situation →	Dog Behavior →	Trainer Response →	Results (Consequences)
Buddy's owner wanted to take him for short walks	Buddy stopped to sniff every four feet	His owner made a loud noise, followed by a jerk on the leash, every time Buddy stopped (noise + jerk = negative reinforcement, avoidance conditioning)	Buddy started walking whenever he heard the noise, and was praised

In Buddy's case, he learned to avoid the jerk on the leash by responding to the warning sound. This is a situation where a knowledge of breeds is critical to providing a solution that is fair and humane to the dog. Bassets are scenthounds, and were bred for centuries for their abilities to trail small game by using their sense of smell. Buddy's owner began using two different leashes and collars to teach Buddy that there were times when he needed to keep walking and times when he could engage in his favorite leisure-time activity, smelling. When Buddy wore his chain collar and leather leash, it told him he would be required to keep moving. When he wore his nylon collar and leash, he was free to take his time and investigate the local smells. Sometimes, even dogs need to take time to smell the roses.

SCHEDULES OF REINFORCEMENT: WHICH ONES AND HOW MANY?

To teach a dog a new behavior, improve the proficiency of a previously learned behavior or maintain a behavior, you must know how to use reinforcement effectively. That means understanding what kind of reinforcement is suitable in a particular training situation, and also knowing how and when to deliver that reinforcement. In operant conditioning, the rules pertaining to how many or which specific responses will be reinforced are called *schedules of reinforcement*.

Schedules of reinforcement define which responses will be reinforced, and how often.

Understanding reinforcement can improve training effectiveness. For example, if a puppy is being taught to sit, should you deliver a reinforcer every time the puppy sits on command, every second time, every tenth time or randomly? It really does make a difference.

Reinforcers can be given for every single correct response, or for only some correct responses. When a behavior is reinforced every time it occurs, it's called *continuous reinforcement*. In training a puppy to sit, if you give the pup a small piece of food for every correct sit, the puppy is on a continuous reinforcement schedule.

Continuous reinforcement is an excellent tool to use while training a new skill, but it should eventually be faded to a more functional level. The ultimate goal of training is to make the dog as independent as possible, and a dog expecting continuous reinforcement will not perform without the reinforcer.

When responses are reinforced only some of the time, it's called *intermittent reinforcement*. If the puppy has learned to sit on command and responds to the verbal cue "sit" most of the time, you might choose to give a food reward only some of the time. This is enough to reinforce the behavior, but not enough to make the behavior dependent on the reinforcer.

Intermittent reinforcement schedules can get pretty complex. There are six types:

- Fixed ratio
- Variable ratio
- Fixed interval
- Variable interval
- Fixed duration
- Variable duration

Fixed Ratio Schedules

In a *fixed ratio schedule* of reinforcement, the same number of responses must be performed before a reinforcer is given. In the example we just used, you might decide to reward the dog for every third sit or every fifth sit, or whatever number you specify.

Some factory workers are paid on a fixed ratio schedule. This is called piecework. For example, if the workers are paid $1 for every 10 items they assemble, they are being rewarded every tenth time they perform the desired behavior.

> Fixed ratio schedules are sometimes abbreviated as FR and a number, so FR4 means a dog is on a fixed ratio schedule where it is rewarded every fourth time.

Some things to remember about fixed ratio schedules:

1. They are easy to use. It's easy to remember when to deliver reinforcement because it's on a fixed schedule.
2. Many competitive dog events have the same preset routines, so fixed ratio schedules can be used to teach the whole routine.
3. Since a fixed ratio schedule is predictable and fixed, dogs learn when reinforcement is coming. That means when several responses are required for the dog to earn reinforcement, the dog may hesitate immediately after the reinforcer is given before engaging in the next behavior.

Variable Ratio Schedules

In *variable ratio schedules,* reinforcement is delivered after a certain number of responses that vary unpredictably. Well-known variable ratio schedules of reinforcement for humans include slot machines, fishing and the lottery. Each of these activities pays off only after an unpredictable number of responses have occurred.

Variable ratio schedules can also be abbreviated. In a VR4 schedule, the number of responses required before reinforcement is given varies, but the average number of responses is four.

Because of the unpredictability of the reinforcers, variable ratio schedules have the power to keep the animal, whether it is human or dog, performing for a long period of time. They are random reinforcement, and we all want to keep playing to see when the next reinforcer will come.

Some things to remember about variable ratio schedules:

1. The animal will perform at a consistently high rate.

2. If you stop giving the reinforcer, the behavior that has been reinforced on a variable ratio schedule continues for a longer period of time than with other schedules.

3. Beginning trainers may find it harder to use a variable ratio schedule. In attempting to randomize reinforcement, inexperienced trainers often spread the schedule of reinforcement so thin that the dog stops responding.

Fixed Interval Schedules

In a *fixed interval schedule,* a specified amount of time must pass before the animal is given the reinforcer. Fixed interval schedules are most commonly used in laboratory settings, often to study the effects of certain drugs over time. The time in fixed interval schedules is usually expressed in minutes. For

Ratio schedules set a number of responses that must occur before reinforcement is given. **Interval schedules** set an interval of time that must pass before reinforcement is given.

example, in an FI3 schedule, the animal is reinforced for the first response after three minutes have passed.

In the real world, most fixed interval schedules related to dogs occur in hours rather than minutes. Dogs fed at 7 A.M. and 7 P.M. every day are on a fixed interval schedule of 12 hours. Dogs that go with their owner to fetch the paper that is delivered at 6 A.M. every morning are on a 24-hour fixed interval schedule.

Some things to remember about fixed interval schedules:

1. They are more suitable for laboratory research with rats and pigeons than in dog training.
2. They are often confused with fixed duration schedules.
3. After the reinforcer is given in a fixed interval schedule, there is usually a pause in the animal's responses.
4. Performance with fixed interval schedules is less consistent than with fixed or variable ratio schedules.

Variable Interval Schedules

Like fixed interval schedules of reinforcement, *variable interval schedules* let some time pass before an animal is reinforced. The difference is that the amount of time varies.

When dogs need to stay on task or behave in a certain way for a period of time, a variable interval schedule might be used. A dog that is not too happy about staying in a crate at a dog show might be reinforced on a variable interval schedule for quiet, calm behavior in the crate. Dogs that are required to work at a task for a long period of time, such as in police or search work, might be reinforced on a variable interval schedule.

Some things to remember about variable interval schedules:

1. These schedules result in a more consistent performance than fixed interval schedules.
2. They require random delivery of reinforcement.
3. They may be harder for beginning trainers to use properly.
4. There are not many training situations where a variable interval schedule is appropriate.

Fixed Duration Schedules

A less well-known schedule of reinforcement is the *fixed duration schedule*. With this kind of schedule, a reinforcer is given after a behavior has occurred (or has been occurring) for a certain amount of time. A biweekly paycheck is one example (although it is often mistakenly identified as a fixed interval schedule).

In dog training, fixed duration schedules of reinforcement could be used to teach the timed stays in obedience competition, such as the three-minute sit and five-minute down. If you wish to teach dogs to "watch me" for extended periods of time, a fixed duration schedule could be used to improve eye contact.

Some things to remember about fixed duration schedules:

1. They are easy to administer.

2. They are different from fixed interval schedules. In fixed interval schedules, the first response after the time has passed is reinforced. In fixed duration schedules, the reinforcer is given if the behavior has been engaged in continuously for the fixed time.

3. In a fixed duration schedule, the behavior must occur for the whole time period to be reinforced. For example, if the dog breaks the three-minute down after two minutes, no reinforcer is given.

4. Fixed duration schedules can be used to produce long periods of continuous performance.

Variable Duration Schedules

In the *variable duration schedule,* the interval of time that the dog must be engaged in a behavior in order to be reinforced changes unpredictably. For example, a guide dog that has to wait different amounts of time at busy city intersections before helping its owner cross the street is on a variable duration schedule.

Some things to remember about variable duration schedules:

1. Like other variable schedules, these are more difficult for inexperienced trainers to use.

2. They result in long periods of continuous performance and do not have the postreinforcement delays seen in fixed duration schedules.

LIMITED HOLD: DON'T BE LATE!

Some dogs work well once they get started, but getting them started is a problem. Limited hold is a principle that relates to both schedules of reinforcement and this problem. A *limited hold* is a limited window of time during which a response will produce the reinforcer. One example for humans is arriving at the airport to catch a plane. Each flight only accepts passengers for a limited period of time. Late arrival means the reinforcer (the trip) will not be available.

Dogs in many performance events must begin a behavior within a certain amount of time after the handler's cue. In advanced obedience exercises, for example, when the handler directs the dog to go out to a specified area for directed jumping, the judge only waits for so long before disqualifying a dog that does not start.

Limited hold can be used to build quick responses.

Limited hold is used in conjunction with schedules of reinforcement to give the animal a deadline for performing. After the deadline has passed, there is no reward for the behavior.

ESTABLISHING OPERATIONS: THIS REINFORCER LOOKS BETTER TO ME NOW

Dogs, like humans, are more likely to respond at certain times to a given reinforcer than at other times. Food rewards are not as appealing immediately after the dog has eaten a large bowl of dog food. A dog that has been in its crate all day may be much more likely to respond to play as a reinforcer than one that has already had several play sessions that day.

The effectiveness of a reinforcer is often described in terms of motivation, deprivation and satiation. *Motivation* is at the heart of reinforcement. If a dog is not motivated to get something (or to get away from something), the item or event cannot act as a reinforcer. An example would be offering a piece of cheese to a dog that dislikes cheese.

Deprivation occurs when a reinforcer becomes more powerful after the dog has gone without it for a period of time. An example is a dog being more interested in food when it has missed a meal.

Satiation occurs when the dog has had enough of a particular reinforcer, making it less effective. An example is a show dog that got a lot of liver treats in the breed ring. When it enters the next round of competition, the Groups, liver may have lost some of its appeal.

A More Accurate Term

In 1982, Jack Michael suggested using the term *establishing operation* (first introduced by Keller and Schoenfeld in 1950) rather than the terms *satiation* and *deprivation,* because there are some other effects that look like satiation and deprivation but are not. For example, water deprivation results in thirst. However, there are some other things that result in thirst, such as eating too much salt. The result of withholding water and taking in too much salt are the same, but it is not accurate to say that too much salt is related to deprivation.

Establishing operations establish the effectiveness of reinforcers at particular times or in particular situations.

Using Michael's definition, *establishing operations* are events that alter the value of a reinforcer. They are relevant in dog training because you must be keenly aware of whether or not a reinforcer is effective at a certain time or in a certain situation.

An example of an establishing operation might be a lengthy play session with a dog's favorite toy just before a training session. That toy would then not be an effective reinforcer because the dog has just had a chance to play with it. Similarly, an active dog that is people-oriented and usually enjoys training may not follow instructions if it has had no exercise during the day and would prefer running over having an obedience lesson. (You'll find more information on how establishing operations are used to deal with problem behaviors in Chapter 17.)

Understanding if reinforcers are effective at a particular time and in a particular situation is one of the most important concepts in dog training. Reinforcement is at the heart of operant conditioning, but you can't reinforce a behavior until you understand what the *dog* considers reinforcement to be.

Reinforcer Sampling: There's More Where That Came From

Reinforcer sampling is one kind of establishing operation. It entails giving the dog a little taste of the reinforcer before training begins. The idea is to get the dog excited and eager to work for something new. For example, you might give the dog one or two improved tasty liver treats before training begins, in order to whet its appetite for more treats in the training session.

The Premack Principle: Grandma's Rule

The Premack Principle, named after researcher David Premack, states that high-probability behavior reinforces low-probability behavior. The idea here is that a preferred activity can be used to reinforce some less-favored activity.

While Premack's work was done with rats and monkeys, the Premack Principle is often discussed in teacher and parent training workshops. In work with humans, the Premack Principle is often referred to as "grandma's rule," because grandmothers sometimes say, "If you clean your room, then you can go outside."

Dog trainers say they are using the Premack Principle with the dog when they train first and have a play session later. But technically, the Premack Principle as it is most commonly taught in education and training settings would not apply to dogs, because the principle requires self-management and understanding what is in one's best interest. However, the Premack Principle can be applied quite nicely to the dog's trainer, who can develop good habits such as training the dog first and playing later.

JACKPOTTING: LET'S PLAY THE SLOT MACHINES

Schedules of reinforcement tell trainers when reinforcement is to be delivered. But in addition to knowing when, you also need to decide which reinforcers will be used and how much will be given. Will the dog get one tidbit of food, two treats or a whole hot dog?

Most of the time, when food is used as a reward trainers use a small piece of food for each instance of reinforcement. In the literature on animal learning, there is some research related to how factors such as frequency, size and delay of reinforcement affect the performance of the animal. It seems to suggest that in some situations involving choice, animals will prefer smaller, immediate rewards to larger, delayed rewards.

Despite this, in recent years dog trainers have begun using a reward procedure called *jackpotting*. Like hitting the jackpot at the slot machines in Las Vegas, the term means giving the dog a large, unexpected reinforcer. For example, instead of a small bit of food, the dog might be reinforced with a large handful of food. Trainers say jackpotting results in an animal that is excited and curious about what might be coming next. However, there is not much in the operant research literature to support this. In fact, the experimental literature suggests that if used regularly, larger rewards can create faster responses in the short term, but the animals stop responding faster when these reinforcers are eliminated.

As early as 1942, the ideal amount of reinforcement was a topic of interest to researchers. Leo Crespi trained different groups of rats to run along a runway. One group received 1 food pellet as a reward, one group received 4 pellets and one group received 16. When they had all learned the behavior and were performing it at about the same rate, he started giving the 1-pellet and 4-pellet groups 16 pellets of food. The result was that the rats ran faster for a few trials. Crespi called this the *elation effect*, and suggested that it caused more pellets to look better.

In another experiment, when rats were given 256 pellets as a reward and were later given just 16 pellets, they began to underperform. Crespi called this *depression*.

The use of terms like "elation" and "depression" is a good example of a scientist using emotional interpretations and cognitive explanations for a behavior. Since there was no way for Crespi to really know what the rats were thinking or feeling, he was also not being very accurate. The terms elation and depression are therefore no longer used. Instead, when describing these effects, researchers call them *positive* and *negative contrast effects*.

Crespi's work suggests that jackpotting can have some short-term effect. In human equivalents, jackpotting is like expecting a card on Valentine's Day and getting a big diamond ring instead. While you might be absolutely ecstatic, the implications for your future behavior are not clear. So it is with the ongoing benefits of jackpotting.

When new procedures are introduced in the dog training world, everyone wants to get on the bandwagon. One trainer told us she was having a hard time teaching her dog some of the advanced obedience exercises, so she was using "the jackpotting method." She went on to describe how she was jackpotting the dog with food every day in every training session. We were tempted to ask her how much the dog weighs. But we did suggest that constant jackpotting takes away the elements of delight and surprise—likely diminishing the value of the jackpot.

Dog trainers are quick to say "dogs are not rats" when they see behavioral research, and this is true. Jackpotting is an interesting procedure for which controlled research should be done on dogs being trained. While animals may appear excited when a jackpot is presented, and this excitement makes trainers feel great, the long-term, lasting effects of jackpotting on canine behavior are as yet unknown. Any result that is observed as a result of jackpotting is not so much operant conditioning as it is the contrast effect. The important thing to remember about jackpotting is that if a trainer chooses to use it, and it is overused, it can diminish the effects of standard reinforcers.

REINFORCER ASSESSMENT: WHAT DOES THIS DOG LIKE?

People are different. We have different preferences about the foods we eat, the cars we drive and the style of homes in which we live. Some of us wouldn't walk across the street to watch a football game, even if the best two teams in the country were playing and the admission was free. Others have no interest in seeing a ballet or visiting an art gallery. As unbelievable as it seems, not everyone loves chocolate. Some people are motivated to earn as much money as possible; for others, having free time is more important than having money. Dogs are no different. Breed differences, learning histories, and specific environmental and physical conditions all play a part in determining which stimuli will work as reinforcers for a particular dog.

When dogs are having learning problems, you may want to conduct a reinforcer assessment. Rather than assuming something is a reinforcer for the dog, you can use a reinforcer assessment to observe and record the dog's actual responses to specific stimuli.

Good trainers experiment with a variety of reinforcers and have an understanding of each individual dog. For dogs that are very people-oriented, the attention that goes along with training may be a big reinforcer. For other dogs that are not so people-oriented, ending the training session may be reinforcing. The reinforcer assessment can be used to identify a dog's preferred reinforcers.

WHAT DOES IT ALL MEAN?

No matter how many times we've heard it, we're still taken aback when someone tells us, "I tried operant conditioning and it didn't work with my dog." Operant conditioning *does* work. There's no doubt about it. Some trainers may not be using the procedures correctly; consequently, they may not be seeing the results they'd like.

Operant conditioning is a science that comes complete with a difficult body of knowledge to master and apply with skill. One book, a few seminars and a video or two probably will not make anyone an expert in operant conditioning. But when there are problems in training, trainers who at least have a knowledge of the basic principles can begin to analyze their animal's performance problems.

The principles of reinforcement we've discussed in this chapter teach us that for maximum effectiveness, the right reinforcers must be identified for each individual dog. The reinforcers need to be delivered on the appropriate schedule. And finally, training is not finished until reinforcement has been faded and conditioned reinforcers established so that the dog can work reliably, consistently and happily for a long time to come.

Canine Reinforcer Assessment

Dog_____ Date_____

Trainer/Observer_____

When trainers are not sure strong reinforcers have been identified for an individual dog, the following assessment can be administered. If the dog appears to be losing interest, stimuli should be presented over several sessions. Some stimuli can be used several times during training; others are suitable as post-training session rewards.

DIRECTIONS: Check each response that occurs.

Responses to Stimuli:	*Appears to LIKE Stimulus*					*Appears NOT TO LIKE Stimulus*			*Shows No Response*
	Looks at stimulus	Barks at stimulus	Reaches for, takes or touches stimulus	Increases body or facial activity	Other	Moves away, crouches or slinks away	Fearful or aggressive barking, growling	Stiffens body	Shows no response or tolerates stimulus
VISUAL									
Flashlight									
Moving toy									
Other									
Other									
Other									
AUDITORY									
Squeaky toy									
Voice: "Good boy!"									
Other									
Other									
TASTE									
Treats									
Hot dog									
Cheese									
Other									
TOUCH									
Pet tummy									
Pet head									
Brush									
Other									
MOTION									
Car rides									
Exercise:									
Running									
Swimming									
Other									
SOCIAL/ INTERACTIVE									
Play									
Ball play: Fetch									
Tug-of-war									
Other									
CONDITIONED STIMULI									
Clicker									
Other									
Other									

Chapter 4

extinction

....

If I ignore it, it will go away

When you're training a dog, you obviously want to teach it to do something. That's where reinforcement comes in; reinforcement is the operant principle governing the acquisition and maintenance of behaviors. But there are also times when you want to teach a dog to stop doing something. *Extinction* is one operant procedure that can be used to accomplish this.

> **Extinction** occurs when a behavior that has been previously reinforced is no longer reinforced, and the result is that the behavior no longer occurs.

As early as 1938 in *The Behavior of Organisms*, B.F. Skinner showed how extinction works in studies with laboratory animals. Rats were taught to press a lever in order to receive food—the reinforcer. When the animals stopped receiving food for pressing the lever, the behavior decreased and eventually stopped.

INTENTIONAL AND UNINTENTIONAL EXTINCTION

Many examples of the effects of extinction can be seen both in dog training and in everyday life with dogs. You can use extinction intentionally to decrease problem behaviors, such as begging at the table or whining while in a crate. Sometimes, you unintentionally use extinction by failing to reinforce behaviors you would like to maintain. Dogs will stop engaging in behaviors for which there is no reinforcement. Changes in a dog's environment can also cause extinction. Some stimuli are naturally reinforcing to the dog, and when they disappear, so does the behavior they reinforced.

The story of Jessie is a good example of using extinction to decrease a problem behavior. Jessie was a gorgeous black Standard Poodle. Her family rescued her when she was three years old. Jessie had no serious behavior problems, and she had a quiet, sweet, calm disposition.

Soon after Jessie came to her new home, she started coming to the dinner table during mealtimes. It started innocently enough, with one of the children giving her some food he didn't want to eat. Before long, Jessie was sitting at the table during every meal, staring at family members as their forks moved from their plates to their mouths. No one cared that Jessie had become a regular meal companion until Grandma was scheduled to visit. They knew she'd be mortified to see this big black dog putting her chin on the table during meals. A local dog trainer suggested a behavior program that involved the use of extinction.

Dog Situation →	Dog Behavior →	Trainer Response →	Results (Consequences)
Jessie begged at the table; her owners didn't want Grandma to see this behavior	Jessie came to the table, sat, put her chin on the table and stared at everyone	The trainer had everyone in the family stop feeding Jessie, and ignore her when she begged (food = positive reinforcement for begging)	Within several meals Jesse stopped coming to the table; she got a treat in her food dish after the meal

An accidental use of extinction is illustrated by Slick, a brindle two-year-old retired racing Greyhound who was adopted as a pet. He was gentle and quiet, and after some time in his new home he began to trust his owner. Before coming to his new home, Slick had not been well-socialized, and he was somewhat aloof around strangers. His owner decided that visiting with new people would be a good way to socialize him, and she started taking him to her weekly card game. He was encouraged to go up to people, and initially his owner had the other players offer Slick a food treat for coming within petting distance. But when she became concerned about Slick's weight gain, no more treats were provided. Within a very short period of time, Slick stopped approaching the players.

Dog Situation →	Dog Behavior →	Trainer Response →	Results (Consequences)
Slick was an adopted racing Greyhound; he was aloof and did not respond to petting by strangers	Slick would go to people only if they offered him treats	The owner asked people to stop giving Slick treats (reinforcement was removed)	Slick stopped going up to people

In Slick's case, because he did not view social contact as a reinforcer, once the food was removed he did not approach people for petting. The food was the reinforcer for him, and when it was removed, Slick's approach behavior underwent extinction. What could his owner do? If Slick continued his visits, the food (a strong reinforcer) might become paired with petting, making the petting a conditioned reinforcer.

DON'T JUST DO SOMETHING, STAND THERE!

Extinction involves withholding the reinforcers that maintain a behavior. In settings such as classrooms, extinction is described as simply ignoring the behavior. When Jessie was ignored for begging, she stopped coming to the table. When Slick was ignored for approaching people, he stopped approaching them. While terms such as "ignoring" and "not paying attention to the behavior" are oversimplifications of extinction, they do paint a picture of how you should act when attempting to use extinction.

The old saying goes, "Don't just stand there, do something!" But to use extinction to change a behavior, you have to think, "Don't just do something, stand there!" That means withholding all reinforcers for the behavior. Food treats are withheld if food is a reinforcer. However, withholding food alone may not result in extinction. If the dog is a social animal, talking to it, petting it or even pushing it away may be just as reinforcing as food.

Classroom teachers will sometimes tell us, "I tried extinction and it didn't work." One teacher described to us the case of Joey, a spirited eight-year-old who caused major disruption in the classroom by making noises during math instruction. The teacher ignored the noises and kept right on teaching. When Joey's behavior didn't improve, she concluded that extinction was an ineffective procedure developed by people who had obviously never been in the classroom. What the teacher failed to realize was that extinction means withholding the reinforcer for the behavior, and it wasn't her attention that was reinforcing Joey. His reward was coming from his peers. The eight-year-olds in his class found the sight of their red-headed, freckle-faced friend whooping like a monkey during math hilariously funny. The reinforcement provided by their laughs and attention was enough to maintain Joey's behavior.

As in Joey's case, if we choose to use extinction to weaken a dog's behavior, we must be sensitive to all of the variables related to the dog's behavior and to any reinforcement—intentional or otherwise—including reinforcement that is not coming from us.

EXTINCTION BURSTS:
IT GETS WORSE BEFORE IT GETS BETTER

Behaviors that are no longer reinforced will eventually stop. However, an important characteristic of extinction is that before behaviors stop completely, they often increase in intensity, duration or frequency. This is called an *extinction burst*.

An example of an extinction burst is what happens when we lose our money in a vending machine. If we push the button and nothing comes out,

The increase in intensity, duration or frequency of a behavior that is not reinforced during extinction is called an **extinction burst**.

we usually push the button again. Then again, only harder. Then we might start rapidly pushing the button and using some fairly strong language. Then we might start pushing other buttons to see if any of them will work. A few karate kicks to the machine, paired with pounding on the front, might constitute the grand finale to our extinction burst. When we finally realize we aren't going to be reinforced, we give up and go away. Our button-pushing behavior for this machine has undergone extinction.

During the extinction burst, the frequency of button-pushing increased as we realized no reinforcer appeared. The intensity of the behavior increased as we moved from fast button pushing to kicking and pounding the machine.

Dogs with behaviors that are undergoing extinction may also exhibit extinction bursts. Such bursts can often be seen when extinction is used to eliminate begging. In begging, reinforcement is on a variable ratio schedule—the one most resistant to extinction. In the case of Jessie the

Standard Poodle, begging was reinforced by the occasional food tidbit tossed to the dog. When her owners decided to stop reinforcing the behavior, Jessie whined. She pouted. She paced, going from person to person at the table. Then she reached up with her paw and scratched her owner on the leg. Jessie's behavior, increasing in frequency and intensity, was the classic extinction burst. Her owners persevered, however, and Jessie did eventually stop begging.

The Price of Giving In

The extinction burst may be the reason some people trying to use extinction eventually give up and give in. By giving in, it is possible to unintentionally "up the behavioral ante" and shape some serious behavior problems. An example is the case of Megan, a preschooler with whom we once worked. Megan cried whenever she wanted to get something or didn't want to do something. In the beginning, Megan's parents tried to ignore the crying. But it got louder and louder, and they finally gave in.

The next time a tantrum started, Megan began the familiar crying. The parents didn't respond. The crying got louder, and the parents continued to resist. Then they thought Megan was turning blue, and they gave in. Six months later, we were providing behavioral services for a child whose tantrums were so severe that she engaged in projectile vomiting when she didn't get what she wanted. Megan had learned that if she made her tantrums more severe, her parents always eventually gave in.

In working with dogs, aggression is sometimes shaped in much the same way Megan's tantrums and vomiting were. A dog that is resistive starts with growling. The owner backs off. Then the dog growls and pulls back its lips. Before long, the owners have a dog they are afraid of and that will snap and bite if pushed to comply with their requests.

Things to Remember About Extinction Bursts

For both dogs and humans, there are several things that may happen in an extinction burst:

1. The behavior may increase in intensity, duration or frequency.

2. Completely new behaviors may appear, such as a dog that starts scratching your leg, pacing or whining to get your attention.

3. Emotional behaviors such as aggression, rage or frustration may appear during an extinction burst.

SPONTANEOUS RECOVERY

Sometimes, when extinction is used, a behavior that has not occurred for some time may occur again. When this happens, it is called *spontaneous recovery.*

For Jessie, the Poodle that begged at the table, begging stopped when extinction was used. But once in a while, even though no reinforcement was provided, Jessie approached the table and started begging. It was almost as if she were checking to see whether anything had changed.

> **Spontaneous recovery** occurs when a behavior reappears following its extinction.

The good news is that because extinction had taken place, the behavior would not continue very long if no reinforcement was given. The bad news is that if one member of the family gave in and reinforced Jessie with food during spontaneous recovery, the effects of extinction would be completely undone. After a long period of time with no reinforcement, if a family member did break down and give Jessie some food, an intermittent reinforcement schedule would be in place. Jessie would then be less resistant to future extinction attempts.

EXTINCTION USING NEGATIVE REINFORCEMENT

Most often, extinction involves withholding a positive reinforcer. Examples include withholding attention from a dog that is whining, or not greeting a dog that jumps up.

In some less common dog training situations, rather than withholding a positive reinforcer, extinction involves using negative reinforcement. In this application, aversive stimuli are no longer removed following a behavior.

For example, some dogs that have been raised with no discipline eventually end up in a dog training class. When these dogs are subjected to demands from owners and trainers for the first time in their lives, they might resist the commands, disrupt the class and, in extreme cases, show aggression. Many trainers will address these problems by refusing to allow the dog to escape the training. When dogs simply cannot escape by acting unruly or aggressive, many will eventually stop their doggy tantrums and comply with training.

In this case, the training is an aversive stimulus. If the dog gets tossed out of class when it misbehaves, then misbehaving has been positively reinforced. But if the unpleasant experience of training does *not* end when the dog misbehaves, the behavior eventually becomes extinct. Used in this way, negative reinforcement weakens the undesirable behavior.

Here's another example. Ruger was a 14-month-old Rottweiler. He was an adorable puppy, purchased by a quiet couple who had never owned a dog. In nonbehavioral terms, Ruger quickly figured out that since no one else was in charge of the household, he could be. Ruger was refusing to have his nails cut or his feet handled. He was described by his owners as an extremely dominant dog, and they admitted they were afraid of him. They finally enrolled him in training class after he bit his veterinarian.

Dog Situation →	Dog Behavior →	Trainer Response →	Results (Consequences)
Ruger was a young Rottweiler that was non-compliant, resistant and aggressive	Ruger would squirm and eventually try to bite if his feet or nails were touched or if he was compelled to follow a command	Trainer started a basic program that involved teaching Ruger a few simple commands; trainer also gently touched his feet and nails, and did not stop if Ruger resisted (attempt to escape was not reinforced)	Ruger began to comply with commands and tolerated his nails being touched

To further enhance Ruger's progress, his trainer gave him small pieces of food for appropriate behavior so that there would be a positive rein-forcement component to his training program. His training continued until he was complying with all commands and was under control. (You'll find more about how extinction is used to deal with behavior problems in Chapter 15.)

Things to Remember About Extinction

1. If there is an extinction burst, the behavior may get worse before it gets better.
2. Not all behavior problems should be treated with extinction. You should never ignore behaviors that are potentially dangerous or harmful to the dog, another animal or any person.

3. For extinction to work, the true reinforcer for the behavior must be identified. If a dog is barking for your attention and you don't respond, barking may stop. However, a dog that is barking in the backyard will not stop barking when you ignore it if the reinforcer is the dog in the yard next door or the squirrels running along the fence.

4. It is important to understand the functions of particular dog behaviors. Many behaviors are used to communicate. Sometimes a dog's barking means, "I have to go outside" or "I am so bored; I am desperate for play and exercise." Good trainers will be aware of the needs of their dog.

5. The reinforcement schedule that is in place before extinction will determine if the behavior will decrease quickly or if there will be a more gradual decrease. When extinction follows continuous reinforcement, the behavior will decrease rapidly. When extinction follows intermittent reinforcement, extinction is more gradual.

6. In training, to keep behaviors from extinction, you need to eventually get to the point where you are using intermittent reinforcement.

7. Extinction can be used as an alternative to more intensive procedures, like punishment, for some behaviors.

8. If extinction is used, it is important to make sure that no one else is providing reinforcement for the behavior.

9. When extinction is used to weaken or eliminate a particular behavior, responsible dog trainers will also put a training program in place that is designed to replace the unacceptable behavior with a new, more adaptive skill. Extinction as a behavior-change procedure is the most effective when it is combined with positive reinforcement and teaching new behaviors.

Chapter 5

punishment

··

Stop that!

Punishment is another one of the basic principles of operant conditioning, and one we must be familiar with if we are to fully understand how behavior works. But it's important to understand that we are talking about punishment in the scientific sense—the concept has a very precise meaning. Punishment involves the delivery of punishers. A *punisher* is defined as a consequence that, if presented immediately following a behavior, makes the behavior less likely to occur in the future.

Punishment means providing consequences for a behavior that decrease the probability the behavior will occur in the future.

According to this definition, if we touch a hot stove and get burned, we can say that our behavior was punished, and we would be less likely to touch a hot stove in the future.

Punishers in dog training include a wide variety of stimuli that, when administered with enough intensity, decrease the likelihood of a behavior. Some examples of punishers include jerks on a training collar or loudly saying "No!"

SOME MISCONCEPTIONS ABOUT PUNISHMENT

Unfortunately, there is a great deal of confusion about the term *punishment*. In our culture, many people associate the word with retribution or physical abuse. Milo Pearsall, an early well-known trainer, said, "The dog is never punished; he is only corrected."

Pearsall was thinking about the word punishment in its cultural context. But as an operant conditioning term, punishment is related to procedures for decreasing behavior. In this operant context, it is delivered with no emotion in order to decrease a specific behavior. It is not associated with getting even, moral or ethical issues, retribution or out-of-control, angry behavior. Trainers who are in an emotional rage are more likely to be engaging in abuse than in the effective, systematic use of punishment.

If a dog owner becomes angry and hits a dog for soiling the carpet, this is physical abuse rather than the systematic, planned use of punishment. If you become frustrated during training and begin screaming in rage at a dog, you are not systematically applying a punishment procedure designed to decrease behavior and are, in fact, guilty of verbally abusing the dog.

Because punishment has such negative connotations in everyday use, it is unfortunate that the term was adopted by behavioral researchers to describe the operant conditioning principle related to decreasing behavior. It is important for dog trainers to make clear the fact that they may use punishment as it is understood in scientific, technical terms.

It is also important to recognize that punishment encompasses a wide range of procedures. When someone says they do not support the use of punishment with dogs, we can assume they mean extremely intensive punishers such as shock collars. But does this also mean they would not correct a dog with a training collar or loudly say "No!", both of which are punishment? As trainers, we need to continually clarify the language we use to describe training and behavioral procedures for dogs. We need to make sure when we are speaking to the public that we are all talking about the same thing when we use terms like punishment.

A CONTROVERSY FOR DOG TRAINERS

A review of the history of dog training shows how the field has changed dramatically in the last 50 years. In the 1930s and 1940s, many animal trainers thought that both dogs and horses needed to be "broken" in order to work well. By the 1990s, the trend has been to use more positive, motivational methods. A controversy has been growing over whether punishment should ever deliberately be used when training dogs. As with any controversy, people have taken positions that range from one extreme to the other.

At one end of the spectrum are the motivational trainers who believe in using only positive procedures to train dogs. These trainers begin training puppies using no leashes and a hands-off approach. One trainer in this group told us she got her Boxer trained to the intermediate level of obedience, but then quit when she had a difficult time getting the dog to go over a jump with food as a reward. "He just didn't want to do it," she said, "and I wasn't willing to start using a leash to make him do things. Leashes are for taking walks."

In the middle of the spectrum are trainers who adopt a moderate approach. They often use positive methods, such as food reinforcement and conditioned reinforcers, to teach new skills. However, they also use mild punishers, such as leash corrections, in order to speed up the training process.

At the other end of the spectrum are trainers who choose to train dogs using primarily negative reinforcement and punishment techniques. There is a belief in some police, military and specialty training settings, such as service dog schools, that dogs must do what they are told and should experience the consequences if they don't work or follow instructions. Many of these trainers would not support the use of food as a reinforcer in training.

We'll talk more about the controversy—and the growing number of ethical concerns related to the use of punishment in dog training—in Chapter 18.

CATEGORIZING PUNISHMENT

As with reinforcement, punishment can be conditioned or unconditioned. Some operant conditioning experts also categorize punishment as positive punishment or negative punishment. Because the terms *positive* and *negative* punishment are being used more frequently in dog training, we will explain them here. However, we prefer to simply use the term *punishment,* because the idea of positive and negative punishment can get pretty confusing.

Positive and Negative

Simply put, if the punishment adds an aversive stimulus, it's positive. If it takes away something, it's negative.

Positive punishment occurs when the behavior is followed by the presentation of an unpleasant stimulus, and as a result the behavior is less likely to occur in the future. Examples of positive punishment include strong verbal reprimands, ear pinches, tapping the dog under the chin or using a shock collar (a punishment we consider unnecessarily extreme).

Negative punishment occurs when the behavior is followed by the removal of a stimulus, and as a result the behavior is less likely to occur in

The Punishment Controversy:

A Continuum of Assumptions, Beliefs and Techniques

Totally Positive, No Punishment

Exclusive use of positive methods, hands-off training, no leashes for training. Use of food rewards. May use conditioned reinforcers such as clickers. Would not use aversive punishers, such as shock, under any circumstances.

The Moderate Position Uses Positive Reinforcement, Negative Reinforcement and Punishment

Positive, motivational training may be a first choice. Trainers may progress from praise, food rewards, touch and secondary reinforcers to snap-release collar corrections and verbal corrections. Might consider using aversive punishers in extreme cases.

Negative Reinforcement & Punishment Model

Basic premise is that dogs must do what they are told to do and should experience consequences for unacceptable behavior. Food rewards are never used. Aversive punishers are used. Many of these trainers are military, ex-military, or police K-9 trainers who believe this model produces more reliable behavior in dogs whose handlers depend on them for their lives.

the future. Examples of negative punishers include putting a disruptive dog in its crate (which removes your attention) or isolating a dog that has been excessively rowdy in a community dog playground.

Negative punishment is similar to the punishment procedures called *response cost* and *time out*, which we will describe in a moment. Because so many different words are used to describe these same concepts, the terms positive and negative punishment can be very confusing. We've defined them because you may hear these terms in seminars or read them in training books. Some operant conditioning experts also like using the terms because they believe there should be a conceptual parallel to positive and negative reinforcement. However, we agree with the thinking of many experts who prefer to simply talk about punishment and then describe the particular punishment procedures used.

> **Positive punishment** involves the presentation of an aversive event. **Negative punishment** involves the withdrawal of a positive consequence.

Unconditioned or Conditioned

Punishment may also be categorized as unconditioned or conditioned. *Unconditioned punishers* are related to biology and need no conditioning or experience to be perceived as punishing. Examples of unconditioned punishers include extreme heat or cold, extreme levels of noise or any painful stimuli such as a shock, a pinch, or forceful hits or slaps.

Conditioned punishers only function as punishers after having been paired with an unconditioned punisher or another conditioned punisher. Verbal reprimands such as "No!" are conditioned punishers, as are sounds or facial expressions that have been paired with unconditioned punishers.

In dog training, in the case of both unconditioned and conditioned punishers, the actual effect the event has on the dog determines whether punishment was delivered. For punishment to have taken place, the behavior must decrease or stop following the consequence. For example, if you yell

> Most punishers can be placed into one of four major categories: reprimands, time out, response cost and physical punishment. Reprimands and physical punishment involve the application of aversive events, whereas time out and response cost involve the withdrawal of a positive consequence.

Types of Punishers

Type of Punishment	Examples of Punishers
Time Out	Withdraw attention Time out (in crate)
Response Cost	Remove toy Remove play time
Verbal Reprimand	Aahh!! NO!! Stop that! Yell dog's name loudly
Physical Punisher	Leash correction (jerk on leash) Hit (such as smack under chin for dropping something) Shove with owner's foot (to stop a behavior like sniffing another dog) Knee in the chest (to stop jumping) Pinch collar (delivers a pinch to stop pulling on leash or aggression toward another dog) Shock collar Other aversive procedures
Natural Punisher	Bitten by snake after putting head in hole

We advocate the use of positive, motivational training procedures when training dogs. The punishers above are listed only to provide the reader with an understanding that a whole continuum of techniques constitutes punishment. Some trainers don't understand that verbal reprimands are, in the operant conditioning sense, punishers, and often they are the only type of punishers a dog will ever need.

"Stop that!" and the dog's behavior never changes, "Stop that!" has not been established as an effective conditioned punisher.

REPRIMANDS: YOU KNOW I DON'T LIKE THAT

Reprimands are verbal stimuli that are used to decrease behavior. Dog trainers use words or strong, negative sounds. Examples of verbal reprimands include "No!", "Stop that!", "Leave it!" or "Watch me!" Some trainers also use sounds such as a loud, nasal "Aahh!" to reprimand a behavior.

Reprimands are conditioned punishers—they become punishers after being paired with another form of punishment, such as physical punishment. Some competitive obedience trainers teach dogs to pay attention by using a pinch collar. In the sit position, the dog is given the verbal instruction "Watch me." When the dog's eye contact and attention drift, it receives a jerk on the pinch collar with the firm instruction "Watch me!" Used this way, "Watch me" can function as a reprimand during competitive events, where no pinch collars are permitted, because the dog has been conditioned to view it as a punisher.

Fixed stares, scowls and frowns are often paired with reprimands, and may become conditioned punishers on their own.

Things to Remember About Reprimands

1. Reprimands should be used to stop or decrease behavior. They are not the same as verbally abusing or berating a dog—behaviors that are unethical and unacceptable.

2. Reprimands are conditioned punishers. To be effective, they must previously have been paired with some other form of punishment.

3. Reprimands can be delivered in a firm, deep voice to distinguish the reprimand from normal speech. However, as a behavioral procedure, reprimands should not be given with emotion or anger.

4. Reprimands are the most frequently used form of punishment.

TIME OUT: ABSOLUTELY NO REINFORCERS

In simple terms, *time out* means no positive reinforcement. In the old days, children were sent to sit in the corner for misbehaving. This was a form of time out. In today's classrooms, teachers often have a time out area where disruptive students are sent until they are calm and ready to work.

In a very broad sense, prisons may be thought of as large-scale, long-term time out areas. Prisoners are removed from a generally reinforcing culture and placed in a restricted environment with limited reinforcers.

> In a **time out,** the individual is transferred from a more reinforcing to a less reinforcing situation.

Time out can be exclusionary or nonexclusionary. In *exclusionary time out,* the individual is completely removed from the situation where reinforcers can be obtained. An example would be removing a dog from class and putting it in its crate in another room. However, removing a disruptive dog from training and placing it in a crate is a time out only *if the effect is to decrease such behaviors.*

In *nonexclusionary time out,* reinforcement is withheld but the individual is not removed from the situation. When you put an unruly dog in a down stay and turn your back to ignore the dog for a few minutes, the dog is in nonexclusionary time out.

Things to Remember About Time Out

1. The dog should not be put in time out for a long time. Usually, several minutes is most effective.

2. When dogs are removed from a situation for time out, if there is no supervision they should be put in a safe, secure area such as a crate.

3. Time out, when used effectively, can be a punisher. If a crate is used frequently for time out, the crate becomes paired with punishment. If this happens, the crate will no longer be a safe, secure den for the dog.

4. For time out to be effective, the original environment must be more reinforcing than the time out environment. In other words, the dog must find the time out less appealing than the situation it is being removed from.

This last point is best illustrated with an example. A frustrated single mother described to us how she sent her son Jason to his room for time out. She couldn't understand why his behavior was not getting better. A visit revealed that Jason's room had a television, VCR, stereo, a closet full of toys, a computer, books, videotapes and video games. Most people would enjoy being sent to Jason's room for a few hours—Jason certainly did!

Understanding what is reinforcement and what is punishment for a person or a dog is critical with time out. For dogs that enjoy sleeping, a time out in a crate may not be an effective punisher.

RESPONSE COST: PAYING THE PRICE

Response cost means taking away something as a consequence of misbehavior. In human settings, when a teacher keeps a child in at recess because he or she misbehaved in class, that's response cost. Late fees and parking fines are response cost punishments that take away money—a conditioned reinforcer for most people because it can be used to acquire other reinforcers.

Response cost involves withholding a reinforcer as a result of an undesired behavior.

In dog training, examples of response cost would be withholding playtime following an unsatisfactory training session or withholding an expected food reward for the unacceptable performance of a particular task.

Things to Remember About Response Cost

1. Response cost is generally a safe procedure. Yet, like all other punishers, it should not be overused. If the dog is losing playtime every day, something is wrong with your training techniques.

2. If response cost is used, you will have to decide when the reinforcer will be withheld. If playtime is the reinforcer, it should usually be scheduled *immediately* after training rather than later in the day. It's difficult for dogs to make the association between their behavior and its consequences, unless the consequences come right away. That's why for dogs the timing of response cost is crucial.

3. Response cost and extinction are different, even though they both involve the loss of a reinforcer. In extinction, the reinforcer that is lost is one maintaining the behavior, such as attention. In response cost, the reinforcer is being used to maintain a correct behavior. It is lost only when the problem behavior occurs.

4. When response cost is used with dogs, the most common reinforcer that is withheld is playtime. But dogs need exercise and play, and if you work all day, leaving your dog home alone, you must ask yourself if it is ethical to withhold the dog's daily play session.

With working dogs, such as those that detect drugs, a short play session is often used as a reward for a good search. If the dog doesn't search energetically, the playtime is withheld at the completion of the search. However, these dogs spend most of the day with their human partners and get plenty of exercise at their work. In addition, the fact that this is a common practice does not necessarily mean it is effective in changing behavior or that it is the most appropriate application of behavioral principles.

PHYSICAL PUNISHMENT: OUCH!

Physical punishment means using any punishers that cause pain or discomfort. Physical punishers are also sometimes referred to as *aversive stimuli* or *aversive punishers*. However, there are times when an aversive stimulus (such as a frown or a reprimand) is not physical.

> Nonabusive *physical punishment* involves the brief, noninjurious application of physical punishers to reduce a behavior.

Examples of physical punishers in dog training include tapping the dog under the chin, an ear pinch, using a pinch collar, jerking on a chain collar or a shock from a shock collar. If used, physical punishment should *never* cause any long-lasting pain or discomfort. If this happens, the dog has been abused.

Things to Remember About Physical Punishment

1. Physical punishment is the most extreme form of punishment.

2. Physical punishment can result in emotional reactions and aggression.

3. Most students who are learning to train their dogs would rather use positive procedures than physical punishment.

4. Physical punishment procedures, even when administered by skilled trainers, are often misunderstood by the general public.

5. The trend in dog training is to move away from harsh forms of physical punishment.

6. Physical punishment can be easily misused by beginning trainers.

7. Physical punishment, in the hands of unskilled trainers, can escalate to abuse.

WHAT MAKES PUNISHMENT EFFECTIVE?

Punishment is more effective when it is delivered immediately after the behavior than when it is delayed. This argues for the dog experiencing the consequences of its misbehavior in training sessions, and against withholding play sessions after training. Particularly with animals, if punishment is delayed, it may not be associated with the response the trainer is attempting to punish.

Schedules of punishment are also important. Like reinforcement, punishment can be given on a continuous or an intermittent schedule. *Continuous punishment* means every incidence of the undesirable behavior is punished. *Intermittent punishment* means the undesirable behavior is punished some of the time. Punishment is most effective when every instance of the undesirable behavior is punished.

For punishment to be effective, it is also important that the punishers selected actually decrease the behavior. Some owners repeatedly tell their dogs "No!" or "Stop that!" with no results. Effective punishers must be paired with unconditioned punishers or other conditioned punishers. In general, stronger, more intensive aversive stimuli are more effective in decreasing or eliminating unwanted behaviors.

THE LAST WORD ON PUNISHMENT

Punishment is an operant conditioning procedure that should be used cautiously. Always start out with the least aversive stimulus. More intensive punishment procedures should be used only by skilled trainers, because punishment can result in dog aggression or other emotional behaviors such as extreme shyness, submissive urination or extreme fear of people and situations.

Punishment should be used only if it has been demonstrated that positive procedures will not produce the desired behavioral outcomes. When it is necessary to use punishment, trainers should provide dogs with many opportunities to get positive reinforcement for appropriate behaviors.

The discussion of punishment in this chapter and throughout the book is not intended to encourage the use of punishment in training. Punishment is discussed because it is an operant procedure, and because trainers should understand that in the scientific sense, a stimulus as mild as saying "No!" can function as a punisher.

Chapter 6

stimulus control

....

Just tell me what to do

Reinforcement, extinction and punishment are three of the four basic principles of behavior. These three principles are related to consequences that occur after behaviors. *Reinforcers* are consequences that strengthen behavior; *extinction* and *punishment* are consequences that weaken behavior.

But to have a complete picture of behavior, we must also understand the importance of *antecedent events*—the events that occur before a behavior.

Antecedents are the circumstances or situations that are happening just before a behavior occurs. In the case of Jessie, the begging Poodle we met in Chapter 4, the antecedents are food and family present at the table. The behavior following these antecedents was begging. The consequence was Jessie being reinforced with food. Later, during the process of extinction, the consequence became the family ignoring the dog for begging.

Antecedents are stimuli that come before a behavior.

When behavior analysts look at antecedents, the behavior that follows and the consequences, the process is called an *ABC analysis.*

Using the ABC format, Jessie's case could be outlined with the following diagram:

Antecedent →	*Behavior* →	*Consequence*
Family is at the table with food	Jessie starts to beg	Jessie is given food

If Jessie's begging was reinforced by one family member but not the others, the ABC analysis would look like this:

Antecedent →	*Behavior* →	*Consequence*
Family is at the table with food	Jessie starts to beg	Mom and dad ignore the ignore the begging; Junior gives Jessie food

In this case, the behavior (begging) was reinforced in one situation (with Junior) but not another (with mom and dad). If this happened, before long Jessie would learn to sit by Junior for all of her begging. We call this *stimulus control*. In operant terms, Junior's presence at the table has stimulus control over Jessie's begging behavior.

Behaviors are under stimulus control when the responses are controlled by the antecedent stimuli. The stimulus will control the behavior because the behavior has been reinforced when that stimulus was present.

STIMULUS CONTROL IN REAL LIFE

In human settings, there are many examples of stimuli that control our behavior. When we are driving down the street and see a red traffic light (an antecedent), we step on the brakes to stop the car. The consequence is that we avoid getting broadsided by oncoming traffic. Slamming on the brakes is a behavior that is under stimulus control: In the presence of the red light stimulus, we stop. If the stimulus is different, such as a green light, we do not stop.

Behaviors are under **stimulus control** when there is an increased probability that the behavior will occur as a result of the presence of a specific antecedent stimulus.

There are lots of examples of stimulus control in dog training, too. In earthdog trials, terriers (bred for centuries to hunt vermin) run through a specially constructed tunnel. At the end of the tunnel, the dog gets close to a rat in a cage that has been placed there.

Antecedent →	Behavior →	Consequence
Hole and tunnel with rat at the end	Dog runs through tunnel	Dog gets closer to rat

In police K-9 training, when a dog wears a harness, it follows a track to find a person. Since police dogs are called upon to track both good guys and bad guys, some agencies teach the dog that when it is in a harness, that's a signal that the person at the end of the track should not be harmed.

Antecedent →	Behavior →	Consequence
Tracking harness is put on the dog	Dog tracks a person	Dog finds the person, and is given food or a toy as a reward

When a hearing dog is trained to signal a deaf owner that someone is knocking on the door, stimulus control also comes into play.

Antecedent →	Behavior →	Consequence
Knock on the door	Dog signals owner by jumping and pawing	Dog is hugged and praised

HOW STIMULUS CONTROL DEVELOPS

When a behavior is reinforced only in the presence of a particular antecedent stimulus, stimulus control develops as a result.

The antecedent stimulus that is present when a behavior is reinforced is called the **discriminative stimulus**.

A *discriminative stimulus* indicates that a particular behavior will result in reinforcement. In behavioral jargon, the discriminative stimulus is called SD, and is abbreviated like this: S^D. In the three examples above, all of the antecedents (tunnel, harness, knock on door) were discriminative stimuli because they were present just before the behaviors were reinforced.

In police work, the sleeve is a discriminative stimulus that signals biting will be reinforced.

When antecedent stimuli other than the discriminative stimuli are present, the behavior does not get reinforced. These antecedent stimuli that do not result in behaviors being reinforced are called S Delta, and are abbreviated this way: S^{Δ}. (Delta is the Greek letter D.)

An S^{Δ} Training Example

In advanced dog obedience competition, there is an exercise called the directed retrieve. In this exercise, three gloves, referred to by the judge as glove 1, glove 2 and glove 3, are placed in a line away from the handler. The judge instructs the handler to turn, face a specified glove, and send the dog to fetch it. In training, if the trainer is practicing sending the dog to glove 1, retrieves of glove 2 and glove 3 will not be reinforced. Glove 1 is an S^D. Gloves 2 and 3 are S^Δ.

Antecedent →	*Behavior* →	*Consequence*
Trainer points to glove 1	Dog fetches glove 2	Trainer gives a verbal correction

Things to Remember About S^D and S^Δ

1. Behaviors will be more likely to occur in the future when discriminative stimuli are present.
2. Behaviors will be less likely to occur in the future when S Deltas are present.
3. Discriminative stimuli signal that a certain response will be reinforced.

PUNISHMENT AND DISCRIMINATION TRAINING

Stimulus discrimination training can also take place with punishment. If a behavior is punished in the presence of a particular antecedent stimulus, the behavior will decrease when that stimulus is present.

Stimulus discrimination training takes place when a behavior is reinforced if a specific discriminative stimulus is present.

The story of Rocky, a sociable Welsh Terrier, is an example of a stimulus associated with punishment. Rocky would approach visitors for petting and social interaction. His family got a new maid and she hated dogs. When Rocky approached the maid, much like he did all other visitors, she started yelling and threw a dustpan at him. As a result, Rocky avoided the maid and attempted no social interaction with her. The maid was the stimulus that signaled approach behaviors would be punished. In this case, the stimulus set the occasion for the response to be punished. This can be abbreviated as S^{DP}.

SKINNER'S THREE-TERM CONTINGENCY

In B.F. Skinner's 1969 work *Contingencies of Reinforcement,* he wrote that to adequately demonstrate what was happening between an individual and the environment, three things must be specified:

1. The antecedent stimuli
2. A behavior
3. The reinforcing consequences

He called the relationship between these three categories the *contingencies of reinforcement.* Behaviorists have a pretty complex system of notation to abbreviate a three-term contingency involving reinforcement. You don't need to learn it in order to train dogs, but a quick look will help you understand the relationships between the categories.

A three-term contingency involving reinforcement is abbreviated this way:

$$S^D \rightarrow R \rightarrow S^{R+}$$

In this notation, S^D is the discriminative stimulus, R is the response (the dog's behavior) and S^{R+} is the reinforcer.

If the situation involved the use of punishment, as in the example of Rocky and the maid, the notation would be:

$$S^P \rightarrow R \rightarrow S^{R-}$$

This means the maid is a punishing stimulus (S^P). When she is present, the dog's response is to escape or avoid her. This is negative reinforcement, and is abbreviated S^{R-}.

GENERALIZATION

Generalization is an important concept related to stimulus discrimination training. *Stimulus generalization* takes place when a behavior occurs in the presence of stimuli that are similar to the discriminative stimulus present during training.

Whether or not they are aware of the technical concepts related to generalization and stimulus discrimination training, dog trainers always try to get behaviors to generalize. Dogs trained on obedience routines in the backyard are taken to parks and other settings to practice, so that the behaviors will generalize to all kinds of settings. Dogs trained for search and rescue work find a number of helpers who have posed as victims in all kinds of situations, and these behaviors are expected to generalize to real emergencies and disasters.

Generalization occurs when behaviors are seen in contexts other than those in which they were originally trained.

Sometimes when dogs make errors in performance settings, stimulus generalization has occurred by accident. In advanced obedience competition, dogs perform a number of exercises in the obedience ring. Jumps are set up for some of these exercises. Sometimes a handler will instruct the dog to go fetch a dumbbell, and the dog will jump over the high jump instead. When this happens, stimulus generalization has resulted in a mistake. The same dog might be taken on a hike later and told "over" as the dog and owner approach a fallen log. "Over" is the command for jumping over the high jump, but the dog has generalized it beyond the obedience ring.

To teach dogs to work reliably in a variety of settings, you must train in a manner that promotes stimulus generalization. This means the dog needs to practice behaviors in different settings, at different times of the day and in the presence of different people and dogs.

Things to Remember About Stimulus Discrimination

1. You must specify conditions for when the behavior should and should not occur, and you should provide discriminative stimuli for the behavior. This means you need to provide clear, distinct signals that tell the dog how to behave.

   Top-rated competition dogs become top-rated because they have excellent handlers. These handlers are consistent in their training, and use body language and their voices (both discriminative stimuli) to let the dog know how it should respond. Their signals to the dog are precise and clear. For example, in obedience, when the handler says "Heel," meaning the dog should walk alongside, the handler always steps off on the left foot. When the handler says "Stay," a specific hand signal is given and the handler always leaves the dog by stepping off on the right foot first. Beginning handlers who have not yet mastered good handling footwork will sometimes say "Stay" as they step forward with the left foot first. They can't understand why the dog comes trotting along beside them. The answer is stimulus control—the dog thought they meant "heel."

2. Positive reinforcement must be selected and provided for the desired behaviors.

3. To develop discrimination, the dog should receive several reinforcement trials with the discriminative stimulus. What does this mean? Practice, practice, practice. The dog should have several chances to learn the skill each day. Initially, gestures and verbal instructions can be paired with visual cues to teach dogs that some circumstances are different from others.

4. Verbal and physical cues should be consistent. We observed one handler trying to teach a toy breed to do the directed retrieve, an exercise where the dog is sent to get one of three gloves that are placed away from the handler (as we described earlier in the chapter). One of the tricks to teaching the dog to do this exercise involves using body language. The handler was trying to send the dog to the middle glove, but it repeatedly went to the first glove, which was placed to the left of the middle glove. The handler became furious with the dog, certain that it was deliberately defying her. Actually, the handler, who was not so coordinated, had lined her body and hips up with the first glove. She did point to the second glove, but the small dog responded to the handler's body placement because it was easier to see.

5. To develop discrimination, the handler must minimize the opportunity for the dog to make a mistake. By using distinct verbal and physical cues, trainers can facilitate "errorless learning." Remember that the saying "Practice makes perfect" isn't exactly true. *Perfect* practice makes perfect. Avoid letting the dog make mistakes.

6. Vary the geographical location of the training, the physical placement and type of equipment, the dogs and people present, noise and activity levels, indoor and outdoor settings, time of day and other conditions to promote generalization.

7. Training situations should be designed to look like the environment in which you want the behaviors to occur, whether it is at home, at a dog show or in the community. Practicing figure-8s in a gym might prepare you for an obedience trial. However, if the

goal is to have your dog behave when company comes, you need to simulate situations such as having visitors knock on a door, come in and sit down to talk with you.

Some great training schools for owners who want their dogs to behave at home have moved away from training areas that look like competitive show rings. They have couches, chairs and tables for students to practice eating snacks with their dogs nearby. Class activities include having owners answer a door to greet someone while keeping their dogs under control. This is done in class, with skilled teachers ready to provide feedback and instruction. Classes such as this set the stage for generalization of behaviors to the home.

8. Gradually fade out reinforcers such as food and clickers and use praise, pats and smiles to maintain as much behavior as possible. Clicking, treating, blowing whistles and spitting food at the dog are great to teach dogs new skills. However, eventually dogs should be rewarded by more natural reinforcers. A reluctant dog can be taught to walk on a leash with food lures and rewards. Eventually, the sights and smells of the neighborhood and time with you should become the reinforcer.

During repetitive training for competition activities, you may wish to continue providing food as a reinforcer. However, the schedule of reinforcement should eventually be thinned out.

THE LAST WORD ON STIMULUS CONTROL

Of all the basic principles of behavior, stimulus control (and the related concepts of stimulus discrimination training and generalization) is one of the most complex and difficult to understand.

Some dog trainers who attempt to read the behavioral literature might feel that concepts expressed with symbols like S^D and S^Δ are too academic to make for interesting reading. But these concepts are essential to a complete understanding of the operant explanation of how dogs learn. These behavioral principles are at the root of most dog training problems and myths. (We'll talk more about how stimulus control can be used to solve problems in Chapter 17.)

We wish we had a nickel for every show dog handler who has told us, "I can't train my dog in obedience. I'm showing him in conformation and I don't want him to sit down in the conformation ring." If these handlers knew about stimulus discrimination training, they would understand that dogs can easily learn to differentiate between the show and obedience rings and the behaviors required therein, just as young children learn that yelling on the playground is fine but yelling in church is not. Different types of leashes and collars are used in the conformation and obedience rings, and these send clear messages to the dog about what kind of behavior is required. Just as verbal prompts like "heel" and "sit" tell a dog what is expected in obedience, a trained dog can easily respond to the handler's command "stand" in the conformation ring.

Many of the dogs that do not qualify in obedience miss the mark because their owners did not provide adequate discrimination or generalization training. Some obedience beginners faithfully attend classes at the local community center week after week. Before long, they have a dog that will perform the beginning competitive exercises with no problems. Excited about their well-trained dog, they enter their first show. After training for weeks in evening classes held in a gym, they show up to compete for the first time one sunny day in the middle of a grassy pasture. Leaving the ring dismayed and ribbonless, these puzzled beginners wonder what happened. "I don't get it. He was working so well in class," they say. The problem is, the dog hasn't generalized its obedience behaviors to pastures and other settings outside the gym.

Beginners aren't the only trainers who have problems related to generalization training. Sometimes, it is difficult for even advanced trainers to provide generalization training for all of the unexpected things that may happen at a competitive event. Who would have thought the ceiling would leak in the obedience building, requiring dogs to work around puddles? No one ever told us we'd do sits and downs in the pouring rain. Where did they get this giant man with a flapping raincoat and funny hat for a judge? And, oh no, I have always taught my dog to do go-outs (where the dog is sent away from the handler) by running to a piece of white plastic fence. This building has no fencing, and they want him to run toward a blue wall.

A larger issue related to dog training and generalization is the high dropout rate in beginning obedience classes. Sadly, so many obedience training classes aren't meeting the needs of the pet dog owner who simply wants a dog that is a pleasant companion and that behaves at home. Well-intended owners sign up for classes at their local obedience school, only to get instruction on heeling and figure-8s. But what most dog owners want is a dog that will come when called and that will not jump on everyone who enters the house.

Obedience instructors who run classes designed around formal exercises think their training will ultimately result in a well-behaved dog at home.

They firmly believe the behaviors taught in class will generalize to the home. But the majority of obedience class dropouts in a 1991 study told us they quit obedience classes because they saw no changes in their dog's behavior at home. This suggests that training is not generalizing the way some trainers think it is.

As we have already mentioned, stimulus control can be mind-boggling. We have presented it here because it is so important, realizing that some readers will wonder what in the world these big words and little symbols have to do with improving their obedience scores or their dog's behavior at home. The main thing to remember about stimulus control is that this is the behavioral principle related to telling the dog what you want it to do.

Somehow, dogs seem to learn despite our inadequacies and mistakes as trainers. When a dog appears to be confused in a training session or just doesn't get it, there is a good chance the trainer or something else in the environment is sending a confusing message. An understanding of stimulus control can help clear up the misunderstanding.

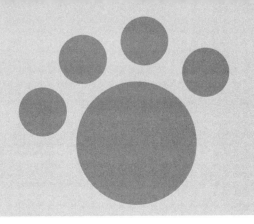

Part Three

behavioral diagnostics: why does the dog do that?

Part Two looked at the four main operant conditioning principles related to a dog's behavior. But in order to have a complete understanding of how dogs learn, we must be aware of still other variables. Respondent conditioning is another process by which the behavior of an animal or human can be changed. Medical and environmental factors can result in behavior problems. Functional analysis and behavioral diagnostics are two tools that can be used to assess behavior problems and determine effective solutions. We'll look at other training issues, too, and how operant principles can help clarify them.

Chapter 7

respondent conditioning

Pavlov and his famous salivating dogs

Operant conditioning is the type of conditioning related to the behavioral principles of reinforcement, extinction, punishment and stimulus control. It is the way dogs are trained and develop new skills. When you give a food reward or teach a dog to respond to hand signals, you are manipulating antecedents and consequences—operant conditioning is at work.

There is another process by which the behavior of animals and humans can be changed. That process is called *respondent conditioning*. It is also known as classical or Pavlovian conditioning, named for Ivan Pavlov, the Russian scientist who first described respondent conditioning in 1927.

In *respondent conditioning*, a neutral stimulus can become a conditioned stimulus if it is paired a number of times with an unconditioned stimulus.

As we described in Chapter 1, Pavlov showed that dogs salivate when meat powder is placed in their mouths. Then Pavlov presented a neutral stimulus (the sound of a metronome) just before he put the meat powder in the dog's mouth. After he presented the sound and meat powder together several times, he presented the sound by itself. Pavlov discovered that the dog now salivated when the sound was presented without meat powder.

In respondent conditioning language, an unconditioned stimulus (the meat powder) elicited an unconditioned response (salivation). In the beginning, the sound of the metronome was a neutral stimulus. It eventually became a conditioned stimulus that resulted in the conditioned response of the salivation.

Respondent conditioning often takes place when dogs are presented with stimuli related to food. A good example is a box of dog biscuits. Dogs can't read, so a box that says "Dog Biscuits" on it is a neutral stimulus—it has no meaning for the dog. Suppose you give the dog a biscuit every morning (an unconditioned stimulus) and shake the box before the biscuit is delivered. The first few times you do this, the dog will take the biscuit and begin to salivate (an unconditioned response). But as the days pass, the shaking of the box becomes a conditioned stimulus. Eventually the dog will salivate (a conditioned response) whenever you shake the box. When this happens, respondent conditioning has taken place.

BIOLOGY, REFLEXES AND BODILY RESPONSES

In both dogs and humans, unconditioned responses have a biological basis related to survival. The unconditioned stimuli and unconditioned responses of respondent conditioning affect the reflexive actions of the glands and smooth muscles. By contrast, operant conditioning involves the striped muscles that control voluntary activities such as barking, running and jumping.

RESPONDENT CONDITIONING OF FEAR

In their classic 1920 study, Watson and Rayner used respondent conditioning to condition fear in Little Albert, an 11-month-old boy. We outlined the experiment briefly in Chapter 1, but to recap, Albert started out with no fear of a white lab rat. The rat was a neutral stimulus. Then, as the rat was presented, Watson and Rayner used a hammer to make a loud noise behind the child. The loud noise (an unconditioned stimulus) produced a startle response (an unconditioned response) in Albert, and from then on he had a fear of rats (fear was his conditioned response to a conditioned stimulus—rats).

What do a rat, a hammer and a little boy have to do with dogs? Many dogs that are fearful have undergone some respondent conditioning that may affect their future behavior. Dog shows are loud, noisy places where equipment is constantly being moved, set up, taken down or dropped. Many trainers struggle with fearful competition dogs that were fine until someone dropped a stack of chairs just as the judge was approaching with a clipboard. More than one dog owner has taken a shy dog to beginning training classes, only to have it attacked on the first night by an aggressive dog. After that,

Respondent Conditioning

Symbols for Explaining Respondent Conditioning

US = Unconditioned stimulus

NS = Neutral stimulus

CS = Conditioned stimulus

UR = Unconditioned response

CR = Conditioned response

Step 1.

$$US \rightarrow UR$$
Biscuit   Salivation

Dog biscuits in the mouth elicit salivation in the dog.

Step 2.

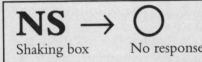

$$NS \rightarrow \bigcirc$$
Shaking box   No response

The neutral stimulus, shaking the box of dog biscuits, produces no response except orientation.

Step 3.

$$NS \rightarrow US \rightarrow UR$$
Shaking box   Biscuit   Salivation

The box is shaken, the dog looks, a biscuit is taken out and given to the dog. The dog salivates while eating the biscuits. This is done several times.

Step 4.

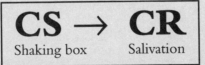

$$CS \rightarrow CR$$
Shaking box   Salivation

The box is shaken, the dog looks, and the dog salivates **before** receiving the biscuits.

Note: The NS is now referred to as the CS; the UR is now referred to as the CR.

Examples of Unconditioned Responses in Dogs

Unconditioned Stimulus	Unconditioned Response
Finger touches newborn puppy's lips	Sucking reflex
Food in mouth	Salivation
Object or puff of air in eye	Blinking
Squeeze or rub outside of throat	Coughing
Pain	Jerking away quickly, flight or fight response (run away or aggression)
Loud noises, unfamiliar intensive stimuli such as lightning, thunder, a screaming person	Fear and startle reflex (muscle tension, signs of stress such as increased heart rate, respiration, panting)
Bright light in eyes	Pupils constrict

A WORD ABOUT WORDS

More and more dog trainers and writers are attempting to teach the concepts operant and respondent conditioning to their students and readers, and it is important that the language be used correctly.

In respondent conditioning, behaviors are *elicited*. This term is used in respondent conditioning, but not in operant conditioning. "Elicit" means to bring about or cause. In respondent conditioning, the behaviors that result from elicited stimuli are unconditioned reflex responses (such as eye blinks and salivation). It is therefore incorrect to say, "I was working with the dog to elicit a sit." Sitting on command is a learned behavior, and the term "elicit" does not apply in the operant context.

Some creative dog writers and trainers have experienced terminology drift, and now use the term *illicit, a*s in, "I tried to illicit a higher jump." Nope. Illicit means improper or unlawful activity.

Another word we've seen used a lot in attempting to describe respondent conditioning is *solicit*, as in, "You need to solicit the response from the dog." We certainly hope not! Solicit means to beg, plead, or approach for immoral purposes such as prostitution.

Respondent conditioning is related to reflexes, and responses are *elicited*. We need to get the language right. To do any less would be illicit.

the poor dog often refuses to go near the training building. An understanding of respondent conditioning is particularly useful when you're working with dogs that have become fearful or whose behavior has changed following a physically painful experience.

IS IT OPERANT OR RESPONDENT?

Dog trainers are becoming more sophisticated, and the demand for seminars, videos, books and magazine articles on operant and respondent conditioning is rising. Some people who are teaching these concepts to others have a sufficient background to do so; others do not. When scientific concepts are watered down repeatedly so that everyone can understand them, the result is often information that is inaccurate.

Some time ago, we read an article on respondent conditioning that used an example involving a cookie jar. The first person to use the cookie jar example was probably correct. But as others tried to simplify the language and put things into their own words, things got confusing. When we read it, the story said, "When a dog sees you rattle the cookie jar and gets excited, respondent conditioning has taken place."

That's not accurate. When a dog is excited, it usually wags its tail and jumps around. These are voluntary activities, and they indicate that operant conditioning has taken place. Respondent conditioning involves reflexes, biology or bodily conditions. If the dog sees you rattle the cookie jar and begins to salivate, respondent conditioning has taken place.

The relationship between operant and respondent conditioning can be confusing. Dogs are complex creatures, and sometimes respondent and operant principles overlap. In the cookie jar example, both operant and respondent responses may be factors.

RESPONDENT TECHNIQUES FOR CHANGING BEHAVIOR

While it is not very useful to be able to condition dogs to salivate (in fact, we're sure some of you would like to know how to condition dogs to stop salivating!), respondent conditioning can be useful in understanding certain types of canine behavior. There are also several ways respondent conditioning can be used to change a dog's behavior. Habituation, counterconditioning, systematic desensitization and flooding are the most commonly used respondent methods.

Habitutation: Get Used to It

Habituation, sometimes called adaptation, is the process whereby an animal (or person) begins to have less of a negative reaction to an event after they have been exposed to it several times. For example, a sporting dog being introduced to field work may be startled by the first exposure to loud gunshots. As more and more shots are fired, the dog habituates and the magnitude of the startle decreases.

For some responses, such as startle responses, habituation takes place with repeated exposure. Other responses, such as eye blinks, do not habituate. The research on habituation also shows that habituation can be a temporary effect, and if some time passes with no exposure to the stimulus, the response may return to its previous level.

> *Habituation* is a gradual decline in the magnitude of the respondent behavior after it has been elicited repeatedly.

This means if a poorly socialized dog is habituated to loud, crowded, noisy places, and its owner then stops taking the dog out, the next time the dog is taken to a noisy, frightening place, it may be afraid again. For dogs that are fearful or easily spooked, socialization must be an ongoing, frequent process to ensure that behaviors will be maintained.

Counterconditioning: Undoing Bad Experiences

Counterconditioning is used to undo the effects of an earlier conditioning experience. In 1924, Mary Cover Jones was the first therapist to use counterconditioning. She worked with a three-year-old boy named Peter who had developed an intense fear of rabbits. Jones presented a rabbit at some distance away as she gave Peter some milk and crackers. In respondent terms, a negatively conditioned stimulus (the rabbit) was paired with an unconditioned stimulus (the crackers and milk). The rabbit was gradually moved closer, until Peter had the rabbit in his lap. By the end of the therapy, Peter was petting the rabbit with one hand and eating a cracker with the other.

Counterconditioning counters the effects of previous conditioning. Oftentimes, the previous conditioning was of an aversive nature.

Counterconditioning is particularly useful for working with dogs that are fearful or anxious.

Systematic Desensitization: Treating Fears and Anxiety

One type of counterconditioning is *systematic desensitization*. Joseph Wolpe developed systematic desensitization in 1958 to treat human behavior problems such as fears, anxiety and phobias. *Phobias* are fears that are so extreme they impair or change the way in which one functions.

In the original systematic desensitization work, people were taught to relax as they visualized situations that produced fear. The imagined situations progressed from the least fearful to the most fearful situation possible. For example, a person with a dog phobia might visualize watching television. Then they might imagine a television scene including a dog. Once they've learned to relax with this image, the phobic person would progress to imagining a dog at a distance on the street, and eventually to petting the dog. As soon as the person can remain relaxed through each step of their fear hierarchy, exposure to real dogs begins.

Dogs are truly brilliant, but telling a fearful dog, "Imagine you are watching television" would obviously not be an effective strategy for changing its behavior. The systematic desensitization procedures used with dogs are called *in vivo* (the Latin term for "in life") procedures, which means they are done in real-life situations without imagery or visualization.

Systematic desensitization has three main components:

- Relaxation training
- A hierarchy ranging from the least to the most problematic situation
- Counterconditioning

A example of the way this is done is Penny, a two-year-old Shetland Sheepdog whose owner wanted to have her certified as a therapy dog. When Penny was 14 months old, she and her owner were entering a public building as a person in an electric wheelchair was exiting. Penny's owner was trying to hold the door open and hold onto Penny's leash at the same time. Somehow, the leash got tangled in the wheelchair, Penny panicked and got pinched between the door and the wheelchair. After that traumatic experience, Penny was afraid of wheelchairs, large carts and other moving things on wheels.

In order to become certified for therapy work, dogs have to behave acceptably in the presence of health care equipment such as wheelchairs, walkers and crutches. A 10-step systematic desensitization program was designed to address Penny's fear of wheelchairs.

1. An empty wheelchair was placed 20 feet away from Penny.
2. The wheelchair was moved to 10 feet away.
3. The wheelchair was moved to 5 feet away.
4. Penny was taken on a leash to approach the empty wheelchair.
5. A person sat in the wheelchair while it was placed 5 feet away.
6. Penny was taken on a leash to see the person, who gave her a treat.
7. The person moved the wheelchair toward Penny, starting from 10 feet away.
8. The person moved the wheelchair toward Penny, starting from 5 feet away.
9. The person moved the wheelchair toward Penny, starting from 3 feet away.
10. The person moved the wheelchair past Penny.

Penny's fear of the wheelchair was overcome in seven 30-minute sessions. Step 6, where Penny got the treat from the person in the wheelchair, is the key element in defining this behavior modification program as counterconditioning. Without this reinforcer, the program would have been an example of extinction of a fear response.

When working with a dog like Penny, you must give reinforcers for appropriate behaviors. The dog should not be coddled or babied with words like, "There, there, you're OK." When attention is a reinforcer, this kind of coddling can easily shape a dog to be even more fearful as it discovers that a fear response makes it owner jump through hoops to keep it happy. Jumping through hoops is OK for dogs, not owners.

Flooding: Sink or Swim

Flooding is almost the direct opposite of systematic desensitization. Systematic desensitization involves overcoming fears gradually, and ensuring that the dog (or person) is comfortable at each level of the fear hierarchy before proceeding to the next.

In flooding, the feared stimuli are presented all at once. In the case of Penny, if flooding had been used to fix her fear of wheelchairs, she would have been quickly taken on a leash to an area near the wheelchair. Almost immediately, the person in the wheelchair would have started moving it close to the dog.

The respondent theory behind flooding is that high levels of anxiety and fear will be elicited quickly, and respondent extinction of fear will also occur quickly. Flooding is a "let's get this over with quick" technique.

> With **flooding**, the dog is exposed to the stimuli for a fixed period of time and escape is not permitted.

With dogs, some police and military trainers use flooding to address fearfulness and anxiety. Flooding was also used by old-school trainers who believed dogs should be "broken." These trainers would not tolerate fearfulness, and felt the solution to a spooky dog was to throw the dog right into the fearful situation and not let it escape.

Flooding has been recommended in the current dog training literature as a way of dealing with fearful dogs. However, we believe systematic desensitization is a much more humane method of dealing with fear in dogs. Flooding can result in overwhelming anxiety and distress. Dogs subjected to flooding often become so traumatized that they lose control of their bladder and bowels. Some dogs resist flooding so intensely that they become aggressive and dangerous for the average person to handle.

The agonizing experiences that can occur in flooding can result in the dog forever associating the handler with the negative experience. Handlers traumatized by a flooding experience gone bad will often give up on their dogs and stop all training.

Finally, flooding teaches no positive adaptive behaviors, and it can easily make a problem worse. "Softer," more sensitive breeds can develop serious behavior problems as the result of intensive procedures like flooding.

THE LAST WORD ON RESPONDENT CONDITIONING

Respondent conditioning is one of the more difficult areas of animal learning to understand, particularly because respondent behaviors (which are related to reflexes and biology) can frequently overlap operant (learned) behaviors.

Procedures that are operant in nature can be respondent if they are so intense that they elicit fear and other biological reactions. For example, shock devices can be operant or respondent, depending on the strength of the shock.

Some trainers recommend putting a mousetrap under some newspapers for dogs that jump on the couch. Generally, this is an operant procedure. However, if the dog manages to get pinched or is so afraid of the traps springing that reflex changes (such as elevated heart rate and respiration) take place, the procedure has become respondent.

Some seminar leaders are now teaching workshops on respondent conditioning. Dog trainers love to be on the cutting edge with new techniques, so more than one dog trainer has told us, "I am using a new procedure to train my dog. It's called classical conditioning." In fact, respondent conditioning is far from new, and it is not a training methodology.

The primary applications of respondent conditioning are in treating anxiety, fears and phobias. Understanding respondent principles is particularly useful for someone who is working with a fearful dog. For teaching new skills or for maintaining and improving a dog's performance, your best bet is to rely on the sound use of the principles of operant conditioning.

Chapter 8

functional analysis and behavioral diagnostics

What's causing the problem?

As wonderful as dogs are, sometimes they have behavior problems. Examples include aggression toward other animals or people, nuisance barking, begging, jumping up on people, destroying property by scratching or chewing, carsickness, shyness, hyperactivity, fearfulness, house-soiling, chasing cars, stealing food or objects, sexual mounting, whining, pulling on the leash, running away, excessive sniffing, digging, phobias and eating the feces of other dogs (coprophagia).

Some behavior problems are really "needs more training" problems—pulling on the leash is a good example. However, when the problems are severe, dog owners frequently turn to behavioral consultants in search of solutions. Functional analysis and behavioral diagnostics are the procedures used to assess these kinds of behavior problems.

CARING ABOUT THE CAUSES OF BEHAVIOR

Historically, in the treatment of human behavior problems, the main focus has been the topography of the behavior. In early treatment models, the function of those problem behaviors was not always considered.

If there was a common criticism of the behavioral approach to treating behavior problems in the 1970s, it was that behaviorists didn't spend enough time looking for the causes of behavior. Using B.F. Skinner's model, behaviorists looked at antecedents, behaviors and consequences. In fact, in the 1960s and 1970s, some behaviorists who were conducting workshops for school teachers openly said the causes of behavior didn't matter; what mattered was fixing the problem. Others pointed out that behaviors could be treated even if their cause was unknown.

Topography refers to the physical characteristics of a behavior, such as biting or aggression.

By the 1980s, behavior analysis was widely used in therapeutic settings for people with developmental disabilities such as mental retardation and autism. In many of these therapeutic settings, there was an increased emphasis on understanding the causes of behavior. By the late 1980s, behavior analysts were using a procedure developed in human services work called *functional analysis*—a process of analyzing the interaction between the environment and a behavior. Functional analysis is relevant to solving any individual's behavior problem, whether the individual is a person or a dog.

FUNCTIONAL ANALYSIS

In human settings, much of the functional analysis research was done with individuals who engage in self-injurious behaviors such as biting themselves or headbanging. Researchers working with these individuals discovered that people engaged in the same behavior had different reasons for doing so. Some developmentally delayed children who were headbangers were trying to get attention; others were trying to avoid doing tasks. Understanding the function of these behaviors was critical in developing effective treatment strategies.

Functional analysis is a way of looking at the operant variables that are related to behavior. Knowing the function of a problem behavior can help determine an appropriate solution.

Behavior problems in humans or animals can be related to a variety of functions. In both humans and dogs, the functions of a problem behavior can be:

1. To get attention
2. To get reinforcers such as food or toys
3. To escape or avoid a situation, such as training or following commands

4. To get sensory reinforcement
5. To communicate needs, such as the need for exercise or to go outside

Different dogs can exhibit identical behaviors, yet the behavior of each dog may have completely different functions. Understanding the function of each dog's behavior gives the trainer a way of determining the most appropriate way to solve the problem.

Two Dogs, Two Different Functions

Jet was a Labrador Retriever whose owner was teaching him to heel. In a businesslike manner, she'd say "Heel," and start walking. Before going too far, Jet would begin dancing around, jumping and trying to get in front of her. He would eventually fall on his back and expose his belly for petting.

Topper was an English Springer Spaniel whose owner was teaching him the go-out, an advanced obedience exercise where the dog is sent away from the handler and signaled to sit. At the beginning of the lessons, Topper would lean against his owner and turn around. He would eventually fall on his back and expose his belly for petting.

Many trainers would recommend the same method of dealing with both dogs. However, a functional analysis revealed that falling on the back and exposing the belly served very different functions for these dogs.

Jet was a hyper "pet me, pet me, pet me," kind of dog whose owner rarely kept her hands away from him. When he was required to work for the first time, he began these disruptive behaviors. They always resulted in attention from his owner. "You silly boy, what am I going to do with you?" she'd laugh and say, as she petted and played with him. Jet learned that his behavior would result in attention. When his owner was instructed to ignore Jet's disruptions and heavily reinforce the heeling with praise and food, the disruption stopped. He got his attention, in the form of playing, petting and tummy rubs, at the end of each training session.

Topper's owner was new to obedience work at this level. She was not too sure of how to teach the go-out, and she was sending mixed signals to her sensitive spaniel. The first few times Topper engaged in disruptive behaviors, the owner ended the training session and started to play. Topper learned that disruption and distraction were ways to escape training. In this case, ignoring the behavior would not have been a good solution. Topper simply wanted to avoid the training, and if his owner ignored him, he would have won the avoidance game. The solution in Topper's case was to continue

Functional Analysis of Canine Behavior Problems

Function of Problem Behaviors	Examples of Problem Behaviors (There are times when these behaviors are normal and are not problems)	Procedures for Addressing Behaviors
Attention	Dog jumps up; increases activity; spins in circles; lies on its back;exposes belly; barks at owner;parades with toy or object; nudges person	• Extinction of attention-seeking behaviors while reinforcing desired behaviors • Give desired attention following training sessions and at other times
Access to reinforcers such as food, toys, bones, etc.	Dog is pushy; sniffs or nudges owner's hands or pocket; jumps upto get food or toy; engages in fast, unprompted behaviors in rapidsuccession (to get reinforced); steals toy or bone from another dog	• Extinction of pushy behaviors while reinforcing desired behaviors • Use reinforcers to reward desired behaviors • Add new reinforcers • Increase access to toys, etc., if deprivation is a problem
Escape—avoid a demand situation such as training or following commands	Dog is disruptive or acts silly; shuts down and does nothing; looks off in distance; doesn't pay attention; no response to commands	• Extinction of silly behaviors • Continue training • Make task easier, reinforce, gradually increase difficulty • Start with short sessions and gradually lengthen • Gentle physical guidance as needed, paired with reinforcement • Evaluate and increase reinforcement value
Sensory stimulation	Watches other dogs walking down the street; sniffs other dogs; sniffs air where people have walked; tracks scents on ground; watches objects motion (such as leaves falling from trees); ignores commands	• In training, remove distractors forbeginning dogs • Reinforce attention to trainer • Gradually increase sensory distractors • Planned distraction training
Communicate (for example, biological needs)	Barks; runs to an area (for example, to go outside); is pushy, nudging owner as in, "I need to go outside"	• Reinforce legitimate communication (such as requests to go outside)

the lesson, give reinforcement for close approximations to the behavior, and use gentle physical guidance as necessary. Physical guidance would probably not have been recommended for Jet, who was trying to initiate physical contact with his owner.

The behavior of dogs is complex. When a dog nudges a person, one function of the behavior might be to communicate, as in, "I need to go outside." The very same behavior might also have the function of getting attention, as in, "Hey, give me some petting!" Functional analysis gives dog trainers a way of examining operant (learned) variables related to behavior problems, so they can develop appropriate solutions.

When researchers and behavior analysts conduct a functional analysis, they collect data on the behavior, systematically manipulate the antecedents and consequences of the behavior and repeat the conditions to determine, without a doubt, the function of the behavior. For example, if a behavior is thought to be reinforced by attention, alternating sessions would be conducted with and without attention to determine its effect on the behavior.

Functional analysis is a procedure that determines under which conditions a behavior problem occurs.

You can use a functional analysis assessment such as the Functional Analysis Questionnaire to identify variables controlling a dog's behavior. The Functional Analysis Questionnaire is used for addressing behavior problems (such as aggression or excessive barking) rather than training problems.

BEHAVIORAL DIAGNOSTICS: LOOKING AT THE WHOLE PICTURE

Functional analysis is useful for explaining the operant variables related to a dog's behavior. Properly conducted, a functional analysis can identify such conditions as when behaviors are maintained by escape or when behaviors are affected by positive reinforcers, such as attention.

However, when addressing and determining a treatment for a dog's behavior problems, it is critical to be aware of the whole picture. That's where behavioral diagnostics comes in.

The term *behavioral diagnostics* was coined by David Pyles and Jon Bailey. They recognized the need for a model that could identify all the possible variables related to behavior, and introduced the technique in 1989 as an alternative to some less-comprehensive approaches for treating human

Functional Analysis Questionnaire
for Canine Behavior

Owner Name_____

Owner Address_____

_____ Phone_____

Dog's Name_____ Breed_____

Dog's Age_____ Sex [ ] Dog   [ ] Bitch   Spayed/Neutered [ ] Yes [ ] No

Any formal training?_____

What are this dog's reinforcers?_____

Describe the problem behavior_____

_____

ANTECEDENTS

1. When does the dog's problem behavior occur?

2. Where does the problem behavior occur?

3. Who is present when the problem occurs?

4. Are there times when the behavior is not a problem?

5. What is happening just before the behavior?

6. Can you bring on the behavior by doing something?

CONSEQUENCES

7. What usually happens immediately after the dog engages in the behavior? How do you react? Petting? Scolding?

8. What do family members or observers do when the behavior occurs?

9. Is the dog getting rewarded for the behavior?

10. Is the dog getting out of doing something with this behavior?

behavior problems. Pyles and Bailey were asked to design a behavior program for a mentally handicapped client who was hitting himself in the face. Before designing such a program, they insisted that the client have a complete medical evaluation. In the course of the medical evaluation, it was discovered that the boy had a cyst the size of a golf ball in one of his sinuses. Treating his face-hitting with a behavioral solution would have been inappropriate and unethical.

Behavioral diagnostics takes into account the operant variables related to behavior, plus genetics, medical status and physical variables.

There are many times when a dog's "behavior problems" will be related to factors that are not operant. Behavioral diagnostics provides a comprehensive approach for analyzing behavior problems that can be used to assess all variables that might be related to a dog's behavior problem.

Looking at All the Factors

The genetics of the dog must be considered when addressing a behavior problem. To begin with, there are breed differences that cannot be ignored. One owner called to ask us how to treat her dog's hyperactivity. She described a dog that never stopped moving. It turned out the dog was a German Shorthaired Pointer, and the owner had no yard, worked all day and lived in an apartment. These Pointers have been bred for centuries to run all day quartering the fields looking for game birds. The dog did not have a behavior problem, nor was it hyperactive. It was simply behaving the way it had been bred to behave.

Medical problems can also affect a dog's behavior. A dog that suddenly starts raiding the garbage or being pushy at the dinner table may have tapeworms; what appears to be a behavior problem is actually hunger related to a medical problem. Medications can also cause side effects that can cause changes in behavior.

Behavioral diagnostics is an approach well-suited to analyzing the behavior problems of dogs, because it is so important to consider the biological variables.

Physical variables must be taken into account, as well, when addressing behavior problems. A dog that is hot, tired, thirsty or exhausted may not follow commands or work well in the obedience ring. Stress can

Behavioral Diagnostics for Dogs

Categories of Behavior and
Examples of Behavior

Behavioral Diagnostics

Determine the cause of the problem behavior, in order to apply the most appropriate treatment.

Genetics
- Breed-related behaviors, such as terriers digging holes, Border Collies herding other animals
- Behavior disorders that are inherited, such as bad temperament

Self Stimulation
- Chewing self or objects, due to boredom
- Running in circles

Operant Variables
- To get attention
- To get access to reinforcers, establishing operations
- To escape or avoid a demand situation such as training
- To get sensory stimulation (sniffing)
- To communicate a biological need ("I need to go outside")

Learning History
- Fear of people, animals, situations due to punishment or trauma
- Past history of abuse
- Past history or reinforcement for behavior, such as aggression
- Lack of training

Medical/Physiological Causes
- Illness, pain, discomfort, such as painful hips (can cause problems such as aggression, refusal to do tasks)
- Medication side-effects

also affect behavior, and there are many possible physical signs of stress in canines. They include:

- Panting
- Pacing
- Shedding
- Diarrhea/bowel movements
- Urination
- Licking the lips
- Coughing
- Sneezing
- Turning away/avoiding eye contact
- Trembling
- Shaking (as if the dog were shaking off water)
- Yawning
- Sweaty paws
- Increased activity
- Decreased activity
- Scratching
- "Spacing out"

But medical questions are not the whole story. The history of reinforcement is a part of any behavioral diagnostics evaluation. Has this dog been abused? Has it had any unusual experiences under specific conditions? Is one person in the family reinforcing undesired behaviors? All the physical and behavioral factors must come together in order to get a really complete picture of why a dog behaves as it does.

THE LAST WORD ON FUNCTIONAL ANALYSIS

Functional analysis and behavioral diagnostics are two procedures that can be used to address canine behavior problems. Functional analysis looks at the conditions under which behaviors occur. Behavioral diagnostics provides a broader picture and looks at why problem behaviors are occurring in the first place. When dog trainers understand the cause of specific behavior problems, effective solutions can be implemented.

Chapter 9

medical and environmental causes of behavior

....

Tell me where it hurts

Operant variables, such as reinforcement, extinction, punishment and stimulus control, are not the only factors that affect a dog's behavior. To understand the complete picture of how dogs learn, we must also consider the environmental and medical causes of behavior.

Environmental causes of behavior are those causes related to a dog's surroundings. Behavior problem can be caused by scheduling or activities, the people or animals in the dog's life, the presence of problem stimuli in the environment (such as a garbage can with easy access) or a lack of supervision.

A BORED BORDER COLLIE

We received a call from a woman who was in desperate need of help with her Border Collie. She told us the dog was hyperactive. She wanted to try a behavior modification program, and if that didn't work, she planned on talking to her veterinarian about medicating the dog.

The owner worked all day. While she was at work, the dog stayed in a crate. When she came home, she put the dog in the backyard for 15 minutes. Then she brought him in the house while she prepared dinner. Exhausted after a day of work, she sat down to watch television after dinner and she expected the dog to sit by her side and be a perfect companion.

What she didn't realize is that Border Collies have been bred to herd. That means they are designed, physically and genetically, to be on the move all day long, working their bodies and their minds. This was a dog that needed some exercise, mental and physical stimulation, and a chance to release some of the energy that hundreds of years of selective breeding had produced.

The fact that this woman, with her lifestyle, ended up with this dog is an all-too-common tragedy. What seemed to the owner like a behavior problem was, in fact, caused by an inappropriate environment for the dog.

The treatment we prescribed for the dog involved spending time with him, having a daily play session and exercise period, and providing him with some basic training. When the owner decided she didn't have the energy or time to meet the dog's needs, he was placed in a home with an owner who understood what kind of life a Border Collie needs. This was one story with a reasonably happy ending for the dog.

SCHEDULING: HAVE YOU GOT A MINUTE?

Dogs can develop "behavior problems" related to their schedule of activities or to the lack of exercise or time spent with their owner. Dogs that have no training and no contact with people can become lethargic from a lack of stimulation. When daily quality time is scheduled, these dogs are less likely to engage in attention-seeking behaviors. Dogs are social creatures, and they need time and attention to thrive.

Scheduling can also create problems with house-soiling. Frequent accidents for which there are no medical cause can often be corrected by more time outside or more frequent walks.

PEOPLE AS OPERANT FACTORS

The people in the dog's environment are really part of the operant factors related to behavior. People reinforce and punish behaviors, sometimes intentionally and sometimes not so intentionally. Children who are permitted to pull the dog's ears and tail will have an effect on the overall behavior of the dog. Loving, responsible owners who give their dogs quality time will most often have a dog that is a model citizen.

PRODUCTS OF THE ENVIRONMENT

Some behavior problems can easily be fixed by modifying something in the home or yard. Dogs that dig up the exotic plants can be taught to dig in a specified doggy digging pit. Dogs that bolt or run away need training and possibly more exercise. But until the training is reliable, environmental solutions may help. Fences might need to be made higher or stronger, or children might have to learn some new rules, such as, "Don't open the front door when the dog is in the room."

Time to Clean Up

We often think of childproofing our homes, but forget to dogproof them as well. Dogs are smart, clever and curious. And they follow the principles of behaviorism. They will try to maximize their reinforcers. "Steak bones in the trash can and no one is looking? Might as well have one." "Dog food bag is right here on the floor and everyone went to work? I'll help myself."

At home, the presence and location of stimuli can be related to behavior problems. Garbage that is accessible will be strewn all over the kitchen floor and then carefully sorted into what is edible and what is not.

Some dogs will urinate on a carpet or piece of furniture that smells like urine. An environmental solution to this problem is to clean the carpet or furniture to remove the urine scent. Problem stimuli in the environment that might cause excessive barking include dogs barking in the yard next door. An environmental solution might be talking to the neighbor about their constantly yapping dog.

In every case, training is essential to teach the dog to respond to commands that will guide it to acceptable activities when problem stimuli are present.

Sometimes environmental solutions to a behavior problem seem so obvious that trainers worry about insulting the intelligence of dog owners when they describe them. But the sad fact is that many people will complain about their dog getting into the trash without ever thinking about putting a tight-fitting lid on the trash can.

There is no getting around the need for basic training when dealing with any canine problem.

You Don't Need a Behavior Plan, You Need a Shovel

One owner called us to ask for help with one of her Golden Retrievers. This dog was eating the feces of her two other dogs when they were in the backyard.

The technical term for eating feces is *coprophagy*. The behavior is thought to have several possible causes. Because some dogs that do this have a medical condition, the first step in addressing the problem is always a complete veterinary assessment. Medical causes can include problems with the pancreas, parasites, intestinal disorders and nutritional deficiencies related to the malabsorption of food. Sometimes dogs eat the feces of other dogs when they are overfed. If the digestive system is overloaded, a large portion of the food's nutrients are passed in the stool. The dog eats the stool to get nutrients.

Other causes for coprophagy are environmental. They include boredom and the dog simply wanting to remove the stool from the area. Some dogs that have house-soiling accidents will eat the stools, and bitches with puppies will sometimes consume the stools of their pups until they are able to leave the whelping box or puppy room.

The owner of the Golden Retriever took the dog in for a complete medical and nutritional work-up. The dog had no health problems and was nutritionally sound. When we asked her about the quantity of feces the dog was ingesting, she described a situation that immediately made it clear she never cleaned her yard. The solution to this dog's problem was simple enough. It involved a shovel and a hose and an owner who needed to work harder to prevent the problem. Remember, if it's not there, the dog can't eat it.

Training was also recommended to teach the dog to respond to the command "leave it!" for walks in the park where other owners may not have cleaned up after their dogs.

OTHER ANIMALS IN THE ENVIRONMENT

Other dogs in the household can cause behavior problems. When there is more than one dog in the family, mealtimes may result in dogfights if the dogs are fed closely together. A behavioral solution, such as punishing the fighting, is one way to solve this problem. Another way uses an environmental solution: The dogs can be fed in different areas.

There are more ways other animals can affect behavior. When there are not enough toys or bones and more than one dog likes possessions, watch out. The presence of bitches in season can have a big impact on the behavior of males. Environmental solutions, such as close supervision,

Environmental Causes of Behavior Problems

Environmental Category	Possible Behavioral Result

Scheduling	• Dog needs individual time with owner
	  ♦ Without it, may engage in excessive attention-seeking or other behaviors
	  ♦ Lack of stimulation and interaction can result in lethargy
	• Dog needs adequate exercise
	  ♦ Without it, may appear hyperactive or depressed
	• House soiling accidents can be related to scheduling

Physical structure of home/yard	• Digging • Running away/bolting • Jumping fence
Presence of problem stimuli	• Garbage—eating garbage • Feces in yard—copraphagia • Feeding close to other dogs—dog fight • Urine smell on carpet—housesoiling
Other animals	• Not enough toys—dog fight • Bitches in season—males go crazy
Lack of supervision	• Car chasing • Destruction of property • Chasing other people • Chasing other animals

providing enough toys and separation as a management technique, can be effective when other dogs are contributing to problem behavior.

LACK OF SUPERVISION:
WHEN YOU'RE AWAY, THE DOG WILL PLAY

Sometimes dogs get into trouble when they are not closely supervised. Property destruction, car chasing and aggression toward strangers can be managed simply by supervising the dog. No dog should ever be permitted to run loose, even if it lives in the country. This is to protect other people, other animals and the dog's life. Fences, leashes, crates and responsible owners are some of the environmental solutions that can be used to prevent instances of destructiveness, going after the letter carrier or chasing cars.

MEDICAL CAUSES OF BEHAVIOR

It is unethical to treat any behavior problem with a behavioral solution if there is an underlying medical cause. Medical problems such as ear infections or a decayed tooth can cause the dog to become aggressive when touched. Dogs that have hearing problems may seem to be noncompliant, when in fact they do not follow instructions simply because they can't hear the commands.

Hip dysplasia, arthritis and other problems associated with aging can make the dog slower to sit, resist changes in position or feel reluctant to play. Internal illnesses can result in lethargy.

A Cocker Spaniel with an Ear Infection

We received a late-night call from a woman with a Cocker Spaniel; she wanted us to design a behavior program for her dog. The dog was aggressive from time to time and had bitten her four-year-old daughter more than once.

As we asked her some questions about the aggression, she casually mentioned that the dog had recurring ear infections. They were sometimes so bad that green pus could be seen coming from the dog's ear. When the dog's ears were infected, it would be "snappy" with her daughter. One of the bites occurred when the child jumped into a chair with the dog and landed on an infected ear.

The woman patiently listened as we told her the most ethical and fair thing to do was to get the medical problem treated immediately. Then she

Medical Causes of Behavior Problems

Medical Problem	Possible Behavioral Result
Ear infection	Aggression, resist touch
Problems with teeth	Aggression, resist touch
Deafness, hearing problems	Noncompliance, does not follow instructions
Hip dysplasia, arthritis	Slower sits, not as eager to move, resists change in position such as drop-on-recall, refuses to jump, avoids stairs, reluctant to play
Vision problems (such as cataracts, Collie eye anomaly, progressive retinal atrophy) or can't see due to hair in eyes or wrinkles (as in Shar-Pei)	No response to visual stimuli such as hand signals, jerk away or aggression when people approach quickly, balks at hand coming over head for petting, problem seeing in dim light
Medication side-effects	Varied; can cause increase or decrease in activity, overall behavior change
Hair and skin problems (such as fleas, allergies, dermatitis)	Constant scratching and chewing
Pain	Noncompliance, aggression
Systemic illnesses	Lethargy
Allergies (dogs can be allergic to fleas, foods, cigarette smoke, fragrances, grass and carpet fibers)	Scratching, chewing for contact allergies; food allergies can cause an increase or decrease in activity
Tapeworms	Pushy to get food or suddenly raiding garbage
Prostate problems	Sexual mounting, bladder accidents
Intestinal parasites	Bowel accidents
Central nervous system problems	Disoriented, confused
Nutritional deficiencies	Lethargy, excessive begging, stealing food, raiding garbage, eating feces

explained she'd already spent more than $1,000 on veterinary bills with no success, and her husband had forbidden her to spend another dime on medical care for the dog.

This is the kind of case that makes our hearts ache for a dog that is clearly suffering. We explained that we could not give her a behavior program because the problem was medical, not behavioral. We then offered her some options. They included having someone else talk to her husband, getting a second opinion or a new medical treatment plan from another veterinarian, contacting knowledgeable Cocker Spaniel breeders who might be able to give her some tips about the dog's ear problems, or attempting to find someone who would donate the dog's medical expenses.

> If a dog has a behavior problem that could be related to any medical condition, the first step in addressing the problem *must* be a complete veterinary assessment.

She was also informed that aggression is a serious problem, and if there were any learned components to the behavior, she was dealing with a dangerous situation. Phone advice for aggression is not ethical or adequate, and she was referred to an animal behaviorist who could observe the dog at home. We also mentioned a group that rescues Cocker Spaniels in danger of losing their homes.

THE LAST WORD ON MEDICAL AND ENVIRONMENTAL FACTORS

Environmental and medical factors can have a major impact on a dog's behavior. To have a complete understanding of how dogs learn, you must look at the whole dog. This includes examining its environment and its health. For many medical and environmental causes of problem behavior, prevention is the best cure. Sometimes just a small change in the environment is all it takes.

Chapter 10

other training issues you need to know about

....

Every dog is an individual

Behavior is complex, and there are no easy answers when it comes to explaining problems related to learning. We've looked at operant, medical and environmental variables related to behavior, but there is even more information to consider before we can fully understand how dogs learn.

Breed differences, the individual characteristics of each dog and variables in the way they are trained, all play important parts in successfully teaching new behaviors or changing the existing behaviors of any dog.

BREEDS:
NO KIDDING, THEY REALLY ARE DIFFERENT

Start making generalizations about any breed of dog, and within milliseconds you will have seriously offended some dog owners. If you say sporting dogs are active, someone will surely tell you that their Weimaraner is mellow, calm and quiet, and never leaves the couch. If you make the point that Labrador Retrievers are known for the ability to learn quickly, at least one owner will emphatically insist that his two Labs are absolutely untrainable. If you talk about the general tendency of terriers to be tenacious, somebody will undoubtedly describe her Scottie as a cream puff.

We understand this because we've owned two dogs that were not typical representatives of their breeds. One was a Doberman Pinscher (typically known as a good guard breed) that never barked at anything. If someone broke into the house in the middle of night, we were certain he would have served coffee and Danish. The other was a sociable, people-loving Border Collie that never read the books that said he was supposed to be task-oriented and aloof. We told people he was a Golden Retriever in a Border Collie suit.

While there are exceptions to every rule, the truth of the matter is that different breeds have developed as a result of hundreds of years of selective breeding for certain characteristics, including temperament. Maintaining and preserving common characteristics within a breed is the whole point of purebred dogs. Working breeds were selectively bred to be strong and active, hounds were bred to use their senses of sight and smell, and herding breeds were bred with the stamina to work livestock for hours at a time.

In *Genetics and the Social Behavior of the Dog,* John Paul Scott and John L. Fuller describe the results of their classic, comprehensive research on dog behavior. Working with Basenjis, Beagles, Cocker Spaniels, Shetland Sheepdogs and Fox Terriers, Scott and Fuller showed that heredity affects a number of traits and that certain breeds of dogs can perform better at some tasks.

> In general, dogs of the same breed share many of the same characteristics when it comes to looks, temperament and behavior.

Certainly there are exceptions within each breed, and dogs that, because of individual genetics or learning histories, do not fit the mold. Yet, for the most part, it is important that dog owners and trainers understand the histories of breeds and specific breed characteristics if they want to fully understand the animal they are working with.

A man who bought two adult Dachshunds, a breed he had not previously owned, was distressed that his dogs had serious "behavior problems." Aggression? No, the problem was digging. And we do mean digging. Left in the backyard when the owner went to work, the dogs soon turned a professionally landscaped yard in an upscale neighborhood into something that resembled a mine field in a war zone.

When we explained that these happy little dogs had a proud heritage of hunting badgers in their holes and tunneling through dirt to flush small animals from their dens, the man found the problem a little more understandable. He eventually "planted" toys and bones in a designated Dachsie digging pit and began keeping the dogs inside when he went to work.

Bloodhounds and Basset Hounds often put their noses to the ground and smell as they walk along. These breeds were developed to trail game by following its scent. Understanding that these breeds are scent oriented can give owners and trainers an appropriate perspective when a dog is taking time to smell the roses instead of heeling nicely. No, the dog isn't being stubborn. It's just doing what comes naturally. One of the goals in training should then be to find a way to make other reinforcers more interesting.

It's All Relative

Because there are individual differences within breeds and one dog may not behave exactly as the breed was intended to, you can benefit from interacting with knowledgeable breeders before acquiring a particular breed or when a training problem arises. Experienced breeders can tell you what is normal for the breed and what the range of variation might be.

It is also important to remember that when general statements are made about a breed, they usually come with an unspoken disclaimer that all generalizations are "comparatively speaking." Someone once wrote that Pointers don't shed much. A Pointer owner who had been horrified and embarrassed in many a business meeting when he noticed vice presidents staring at all the short white hairs on his dark suit disagreed. For him, Pointers do shed a lot. It's all relative.

A Word About Mixed Breeds

Mixed-breed dogs are a mixture of more than one breed. Sometimes, knowing the breeds that contributed to the dog's ancestry will provide some valuable information about the best way to train the dog. But you do not always have the luxury of knowing the background of mixed-breed dogs— sometimes so many breeds have been intermixed for so many generations that it would be impossible to tell. When the background is unknown, sound behavioral principles are all we have left to train the dog.

TRAINABILITY:
A DANDIE DINMONT IS NOT A MASTIFF

In general, some breeds learn faster by traditional training methods than others. The important thing to remember is that dogs of every breed have been trained to the advanced levels of obedience by skilled trainers. Some breeds are more challenging to train, and they are seen in formal competition less often. But having a breed that is not often seen in the obedience ring should never be an excuse for lack of training. When operant conditioning procedures are applied correctly, all dogs can learn.

At a very large dog show, we observed a wide variety of breeds as they went through the Canine Good Citizen test—a test of basic training and good manners that was developed by the American Kennel Club. During testing, owners are not permitted to force dogs into positions, but they may give minimal physical prompts to cue their dog. For example, if a dog does not sit with the first verbal command, the owner can gently give some physical guidance. Many owners at the show entered their dogs in the test even though the dogs had received no formal training. Some of the dogs had never been taught to sit on command. Yet in many cases, with many breeds, if owners gave some gentle guidance, the dogs would sit anyway.

It was interesting to see that some breeds resisted being guided into position. In particular, all of the Chinese Shar-Pei would spring back into a standing position when their owners tried to guide them to sit. Later, we heard from several trainers who were skilled at using clickers as secondary reinforcers that they had little success using clickers with Shar-Pei.

Does this mean that Shar-Pei are untrainable? Of course not. What it means is that trainers need to find out what makes this breed (and individual dogs within the breed) tick. A Shar-Pei that we knew would sit for long periods of time and watch television. The same dog would sit in front of a full-length mirror and turn her head from side to side, as if she were checking her lipstick. This dog was visually oriented. She was stoic and not impressed with our offers of the standard reinforcers.

A knowledge of specific breeds can give you an edge when it comes to selecting reinforcers and training methods that best suit a particular dog.

INDIVIDUAL EXCEPTIONS: THERE'S ONE IN EVERY BUNCH

In addition to understanding specific aspects of particular breeds, good trainers are in tune with the unique characteristics of the individual dogs they are working with. Just as people have individual learning styles and preferences based on their biology and learning histories, the idea of "different strokes for different folks" also applies to dogs.

Even after major medical issues have been ruled out, some dogs have complications related to physiology that can influence learning. For example, hyperactivity can be present in dogs as well as children, although this diagnosis should be made carefully by a veterinarian and not misapplied to a dog that is simply very active.

Some dogs are not reinforced by the same things that other dogs respond to. To them, it's "Treats and food—who cares?" Other dogs couldn't care less about praise, and the many "Good boys!" squealed by owners throughout a training session may go in one ear and out the other.

In addition, some individuals within a breed may be less responsive to verbal instructions than others, and some dogs are much more visually oriented than you might realize. Individual dogs within a litter can have temperament problems, and dogs from the same breeding lines can have particular characteristics, such as aggression toward people or animals.

WHAT MAKES A GOOD DOG TRAINER?

Considering everything competent dog trainers must know, training a dog sounds like a complicated process. Two of the most critical steps in the training process are developing an understanding of the individual dog and taking a careful look at the behaviors that are present. These two steps will provide a starting point for successful training.

If there were a mathematical formula for dog training, the dog would make up one half of the equation and the trainer would undoubtedly account for the other half. The behavior and skills of the person working with a dog will have a significant impact on the dog's ability to learn. Being able to analyze your own behavior as a trainer is an important part of understanding how dogs learn.

A few years ago, in a seminar for professionals who work with autistic children, a leading therapist was asked what she looked for when she interviewed staff for her clinic. As most of the seminar audience grabbed their pens and prepared to record a long list of behavioral skills, this very behaviorally oriented expert gave a response that was dramatically simple: "The ability to be kind and to persevere." She went on to say that she could teach anyone the other technical skills required to be a good teacher.

These thoughts could just as easily be applied to dog training. Some trainers have good intentions, but they have a difficult time developing a kindness toward the dogs they are teaching because of some common misconceptions about how dogs think and learn. One trainer who was being downright mean and verbally abusive to her toy dogs had been shamefully misled by her instructor. He filled her head with the notion that dogs deliberately misbehave in training in order to "get back at" the trainer. "That dog's too smart," he'd tell her. "She is deliberately trying to pull your chain."

Trainer Observation Form

Trainer_____Observer_____Date_____

Trainer Behavior	Looks Good	Needs Improvement (Inconsistent)	Consistently a Problem
I. GENERAL			
A. Selection of Goal/Task to be Trained			
1. Identified appropriate goal for dog (physical condition, prerequisite skills)_____			
2. Tasks trained in			
• small enough steps_____			
• logical sequence_____			
• trainer is organized (materials present, set up)			
B. Appropriate Length of Training Session			
1. Specific tasks change often enough_____			
2. End on positive note—quit while still fun			
C. Training Is Fun, Stimulating for Dog			
II. APPLICATION OF OPERANT PRINCIPLES			
A. Delivery of Reinforcers			
1. Appropriate reinforcer selected (dog likes it)_____			
2. Timing of reinforcement			
• reinforcer delivered immediately_____			
• not too soon_____			
• not too late_____			
3. Consistency			
• reinforces desired new behavior consistently_____			
• inappropriate behaviors not reinforced__			
4. Schedule of reinforcement			
• applies appropriate schedule_____			
• fades reinforcers from continuous to variable when dog learns skill_____			
5. Appropriate size of reinforcement_____			
6. Attention_____			
7. Secondary reinforcement used appropriately			
• clicker (if applicable)_____			
• praise_____			
• other_____			

Trainer Behavior	Looks Good	Needs Improvement (Inconsistent)	Consistently a Problem
B. Stimulus Control			
1. Trainer consistent with			
• hand signals_____			
• footwork_____			
• body language_____			
• verbal instructions/prompts_____			
• not overly verbal_____			
• appropriate quality of voice (tone, loudness)_____			
2. Use of visual cues is appropriate (tape to mark go-out pattern, etc.)_____			
3. Cues faded at appropriate pace			
• gradually_____			
• not too fast			
III. BEHAVIOR PROBLEMS			
A. Behavioral Diagnostics, Functional Analysis			
1. Trainer has ruled out medical problems_____			
2. Implements environmental solutions as needed_____			
3. Functional analysis to identify conditions under which behavior occurs_____			
B. Maladaptive Behaviors			
1. Humane treatment strategy selected_____			
2. Behaviors reduced while reinforcing appropriate behaviors, new skills_____			
3. Respondent behaviors handled appropriately			
C. Punishment (Used only after positive procedures have been tried. See definition, which includes verbal corrections.)			
1. Trainer does not punish appropriate behaviors_____			
2. If punishers are used			
• appropriate level of punishment is used_____			
• humane, delivered with no emotion_____			
• appropriate behavior consistently reinforced_____			
• return to positive procedures as soon as possible_____			
3. Other			
IV. TRAINER ATTITUDE AND DEMEANOR			
1. Trainer has a positive, upbeat, demeanor_____			
2. Would you like this person to teach you how to do something?			
V. OTHER COMMENTS AND SUGGESTIONS			

Other trainers use different terms to express the same idea. "That dog enjoys pushing you around," they might say. Nothing could be further from the truth. Deception and manipulation are simply not part of a dog's repertoire of behaviors. Dogs are incapable of those feelings.

Another trainer was trying to teach his dog to do the drop on recall. This is an obedience exercise in which the handler calls the dog. As the dog is coming, it is signaled to drop into a down position with a voice or hand signal. Then, at the judge's instruction, the dog is called to come and sit in front of the handler. A common mistake dogs make in this exercise is to anticipate the second recall. After dropping, they get up unprompted and return to the owner, thereby earning a disqualifying score. The trainer we observed was using water balloons to correct a Golden Retriever that had been anticipating the recall. At one point, the dog was in the down position doing everything exactly right. From nowhere, the trainer hurled a water balloon at the dog and hit him. "Why did you do that; he was doing it right!" we exclaimed. The trainer's response was, "I didn't want him to even think about doing it wrong." In other words, the dog was being punished for engaging in the correct behavior.

Dogs are not so complex as to try to get back at their trainers. They would much rather be treated with fairness and consistent rules. You can create learning problems when you punish appropriate behaviors (as in the case of the water balloons) and when you give mixed signals. Dogs punished inconsistently often become so fearful that they are reluctant to engage in any behavior because they are expecting a punisher. Some toy breeds will sit and quiver, lifting a submissive paw in the air as they appear to completely shut down.

In the laboratory there is a saying, "The rat is always right." What this means is that the rat always responds according to behavioral principles. In dog training, the dog is always right. If a dog appears to be goofing off and acting silly during training, it means training has not been established as a reinforcing activity. The item chosen as a reinforcer may not be reinforcing to that dog, or you may not be delivering the reinforcer frequently enough. You may be sending confusing messages with inconsistent footwork or body language. If punishment is used, you may be inadvertently punishing appropriate behaviors.

A trainer with a sound knowledge of breeds, a sensitivity and understanding of individual dogs, and competence in operant conditioning and the application of behavioral principles, can build a bond with a dog that is wonderful, intense and almost magical. For the rest of us, the Trainer

Observation Form provides a checklist of human behaviors that can be used to identify trainer-related problems.

When you're using this form, you'll need someone skilled in dog training to observe you working with your dog. You may need to be observed more than once in order to identify any problem areas. And, as with any training problem, a thorough veterinary examination should be made to rule out any canine health problems.

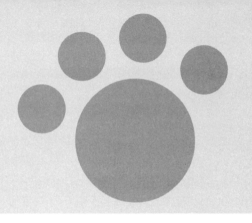

Part Four

increasing behaviors: teaching your old dog new tricks

....

When you want to teach your dog something new, there are several techniques you can use that are based on the principles of operant conditioning. These procedures are shaping, fading, chaining and conditioned reinforcement. Shaping, fading and chaining are the operant principles that must be applied in any situation where the dog is expected to learn a new skill. Conditioned reinforcement, which we introduced in Chapter 3, is what makes the training rewarding.

Chapter 11

shaping

··

You're getting warmer

The children in Ola Mae Douglas's third-grade class at North Shore Elementary School didn't know it, but they were using shaping to change the behavior of their friend and classmate. During free time at recess, the children were playing Hot and Cold, and they had Billy Johnson looking everywhere for a hidden tennis ball.

As he got nearer to the ball, the children said, "You're getting warmer." If he wandered away, they said, "You're getting colder." When Billy was close to the ball, the excitement picked up and everyone chimed in, "You're getting hot." Finally, as their reinforcement for going in the right direction led Billy to the hiding spot, the delighted children screamed, "You're burning up!"

Shaping is a process used to establish a new behavior. To teach the concept, instructors often use an adult version of Hot and Cold. In this game, a person leaves the room and the group decides on a behavior to be shaped, such as walking to the chalkboard, drawing a circle and putting one's nose in the circle.

The person returns to the room, clueless about what has been decided. He or she behaves randomly, trying to guess what is required. The designated trainer reinforces close approximations to the desired behavior with a whistle or clicker. Usually, in a very short time, the person is standing with his or her nose in a chalk circle drawn on the board and a room full of students have witnessed the power of shaping.

Dog trainers can learn a lot from the way humans behave in the shaping game. First, some people in the game are better "animals" than others.

Shaping is reinforcing successive approximations of a desired behavior. Successive approximations are any behaviors that get the individual closer to the desired behavior, or any behaviors that resemble the desired behavior.

They move about freely and engage in plenty of behavior that can be reinforced. Others, shy, embarrassed and unsure about what they are supposed to do, are reluctant to move in one direction or another. The same variation in responses can be seen in dogs. Some will perform a wide variety of behaviors as quickly as possible, almost as if they are trying to guess what they must do to earn a reward. Other dogs will shut down before your very eyes, seemingly afraid to try anything new. Trainers who try the shaping game with their dogs quickly learn that individual animals of the same species can be very different.

The shaping game also makes us aware of the tendency for many of us to be too verbally oriented when we try to teach something. Many trainers attempt to teach both dogs and humans with words, explanations and more words. But because dogs don't do so well with lectures, their ability to learn new tasks will ultimately depend on your ability to use shaping.

HOW SHAPING WORKS

Does it seem counterintuitive to reinforce a behavior that is not exactly what you want? Why not wait until the dog gets it right before you reinforce its behavior? Because animals don't always engage in the desired behavior on their own. For example, if the goal were to train a rabbit to play a toy piano, a trainer aware of the principles of reinforcement might say, "Well, I would reinforce the rabbit only when it played the piano." Good idea, but what happens when the rabbit doesn't go near the piano?

Shaping is one way to get the rabbit into position. (It's also a much more humane way than forcing a confused bunny into position at a piano.) The rabbit and the piano would be put in a confined space. When the rabbit made its first random moves toward the piano, the behavior would be reinforced. As the rabbit moved a step closer, it would be reinforced again, and so on, until it was near the piano. Next the rabbit might be reinforced for sitting up in front of the piano, then for placing its front paws on the keys. Before the trainer knows what has happened, the melodic sounds of *Here Comes Peter Cottontail* are floating through the air and shaping has taken place.

THE ULTIMATE TEACHING TOOL

Marian Breland Bailey and Bob Bailey of Animal Behavior Enterprises have used shaping and other behavioral principles to train nearly 140 species of animals. Think your Afghan Hound will never get that coveted Utility title? Take heart! The Baileys have shown that shaping can be used to teach apes, whales, dolphins and pigs. You already knew those animals were smart? Well, they've also used shaping to teach hamsters, chickens, vultures, albatrosses, emus, lizards, frogs, sea horses, bluegill fish, squid, rock crabs and cockroaches.

Bob Bailey and Marian Breland Bailey have trained more than 140 species of animals using operant conditioning procedures such as shaping.

DOG TRAINING IS ALWAYS SHAPING

The ability to use shaping is critical in teaching dogs new skills. Many trainers routinely use shaping procedures, even though they may not be aware of the technical term for what they are doing.

Shaping can be used in dog training to teach a variety of new skills.

In agility and obedience, for example, dogs are required to go over jumps. For bigger dogs, the jumps may be as high as three feet. To introduce dogs to jumping, trainers often start with low jumps and gradually raise them. These are successive approximations of the final behavior—a shaping procedure.

A program for teaching a novice dog to jump might go something like this:

1. The dog is walked on a leash through the two upright poles (stanchions) that hold the jump, and is rewarded.
2. A bar is placed at ground level between the stanchions, and the dog is walked over the bar on a leash. As the dog steps over the bar, the trainer gives the command "Jump" and then rewards the dog.
3. The bar is raised a few inches off the ground, and the dog is taken over as it is told "Jump." Then the dog is rewarded.
4. The bar is raised to one foot off the ground, and the dog is told "Jump." It is rewarded after the jump.

The shaping process continues until the dog is jumping the desired height. Each trial is reinforced, and eventually the leash and the trainer are no longer used.

Steps in Shaping

1. Identify the desired behavior (in the previous example, the dog goes over the high jump).
2. Identify the response that can be used to begin shaping (the dog steps through the stanchions).
3. Reinforce the beginning response.
4. Gradually require closer approximations to the final behavior, reinforcing each one, until the goal is reached.

Things to Remember About Shaping

1. Shaping can be used to:

   - Change the form of a behavior, such as shaping a whine into a bark that the dog uses to signal it needs to go out.
   - Increase the frequency of a behavior.
   - Affect the time related to a behavior, such as speeding up a response.
   - Change the intensity of a behavior, such as teaching a dog to push hard enough on the equipment to release the ball in a flyball box.

2. Shaping is a powerful behavioral tool. It should never be used to push a dog beyond reasonable limits, such as jumping too high.

3. For shaping to be effective, you must not move too quickly from one approximation of the desired behavior to the next. Make sure each step is firmly established before proceeding.

4. Move through the shaping process in small steps, but do not make the steps so small that training becomes boring.

5. If the dog fails at one level, return to an easier step.

6. Consistently reinforce success at each step of the shaping process.

Chapter 12

prompting and fading

Can you give me a hint?

Show us someone who watches a dog with advanced training and says, "My dog could never do that," and we'll show you someone who doesn't understand prompting and fading.

Prompting and *fading* are the behavioral version of what's happening behind the scenes in a magic act. No Virginia, the young woman in the magic act doesn't really levitate off the table; she is on the very well-disguised arm of a forklift. The well-trained dog has had the benefit of hours of good training. That training was partly made up of prompts and fading that, like the forklift, could not be seen in the final presentation.

A TIME AND PLACE FOR EVERYTHING

Once you have used shaping to teach new behaviors and differential reinforcement to increase those behaviors, you need a way to ensure the behaviors will occur at the right time and place. That's where prompting and fading come in: They are used to get target behaviors to occur reliably in the appropriate settings and situations.

> **Prompting** means providing antecedents that result in the occurrence of a target behavior.

Prompts increase the likelihood that the dog (or person) will engage in the correct behavior at the right time and place. We think of them as hints or extra help in showing the dog what you expect.

Response Prompts

One category of prompts is offered directly by your behavior. In other words, something you do acts as a prompt. These are called *response prompts*. Examples include:

- Verbal prompts, as when you stand by the broad jump and say to the dog, "Over."
- Gestural prompts, as when you wave your hand over the jump or point to the jump.
- Physical prompts, as when you hold the leash or collar and guide the dog over the jump.
- Modeling prompts, as when you go over the jump first, with the dog following behind on a leash.

Modeling is used much less with dogs than in human training settings. Most trainers would not teach jumping by going over a jump themselves—although some do!

Environmental Prompts

Prompts can also be related to stimuli. These kinds of prompts are called *environmental* or *stimulus prompts*. An environmental prompt involves adding or removing a stimulus to increase the likelihood of getting the correct response. For example, in the exciting dog sport called flyball, dogs are required to run, jump over a series of low jumps, press a lever on a box that tosses a ball, catch the ball and return to their handler over the jumps. The sport is run as a relay race, with two teams and two sets of equipment placed side by side. Dogs love flyball, and they move at lightning speeds in furry blurs as the crowd screams and cheers.

Some dogs that are learning flyball have problems when they are first sent to go over the jumps without their handler. They take a few steps, run around the jumps or wander off the course to see other dogs or smell something in the training area. To prevent this, some flyball trainers construct a chute out of boards standing on their sides to guide the dog from the handler to the first jump. The chute is an environmental prompt that increases the likelihood the dog will go over the first jump.

FADING: WEANING OFF THE SPECIAL HELP

With this flyball example, entry chutes work well for beginning dogs, but the dog must eventually be able to work without special prompts. Trainers who use the chutes to teach flyball gradually move the boards wider and wider apart, or they gradually add open spaces in the chute until the boards are completely removed. This procedure is an example of *fading*.

> *Fading* means gradually reducing the strength of a prompt.

You can use fading in several ways:

- Fading verbal prompts from louder commands to whispers.
- Fading environmental prompts, such as special training equipment or modifications.
- Fading physical prompts, such as initially using a leash to guide the dog and eventually removing the leash.
- Fading one prompt when two are used during training, such as starting with hand signals and verbal commands, and fading to hand signals only.

Things to Remember About Fading

1. Before using fading, you must decide what you want the dog's final behavior to be.
2. You should identify the prompts to be faded and have a plan for fading them.
3. Cues should be faded so gradually that mistakes are avoided and the dog has what we call *errorless learning*.
4. If the dog does make a mistake, move back to the previous level and bring back the more intense level of prompts.

TRANSFER OF STIMULUS CONTROL

Fading prompts is how you transfer stimulus control. This means that stimulus control is transferred from the environmental stimuli (such as verbal and physical help or special training equipment) to the natural, final stimulus related to the desired behavior.

Examples of Fading in Formal Obedience Training

Activity/Exercise	Method of Fading
Lie Down	Start with leash on and dog in sit position. Facing dog, say "down," and with a large forward motion of the arm push down on the leash until dog is in the down position. Repeat, gradually **fading** the verbal and physical prompt and stepping back until the dog responds to the hand signal only.
Heel	Leash is **faded** from Novice to off-leash work in Open and Utility classes. A short, very light cord may be used as a transition from leash to no leash.
Figure Eight	Same as with Heel.
Stand for Judge's Exam	Begin with dog in sit position. Hand signal to stand is paired with verbal command "stand." In the beginning, the handler uses a physical prompt. The handler holds the dog's collar to guide the dog from sit to stand, and a hand under the belly holds the dog in the stand if needed. Physical prompts are gradually **faded**.
Recall (dog called to handler)	Dog is taught to come from a short distance on a leash. Slight tug on the leash is paired with verbal command "come." The leash is **faded**.
Directed Jumping (dog signaled by handler to go over one of two jumps)	Initially, the handler stands right at the jump the dog is to go over. Handler gradually moves away (**fades** presence at jump) and the dog is signaled from a distance.

How does this work? A good example is the sit front exercise in obedience competition. In this exercise, when the dog is called to come it must return to the handler and sit down straight in front, looking up at the handler. Many trainers use wooden dowels to guide the dog into the correct front-and-center position—physical prompts. The dowels can eventually be shortened, then removed, and the handler can cue the dog with two index fingers pointing downward to indicate "front." Finally, unless the handler wishes to be disqualified from formal obedience competition, pointing with the fingers must be faded and the hands must hang naturally at the handler's sides. Stimulus control has been transferred from the dowels to the handler's pointing fingers to the final stimulus of the handler standing in a natural position.

All this has been achieved using prompts and fading. It's how old dogs learn new tricks. Special training aids are faded, physical guidance of the dog is faded to verbal instructions, and the trainer holds off on hinting and helping for longer periods of time.

THE LAST WORD ON PROMPTING AND FADING

Because humans are verbal, schoolteachers often begin with the lowest level of prompts. They start with verbal prompts and increase to physical prompts

> You transfer stimulus control by decreasing the level of prompts from most to least, decreasing physical guidance and delaying the time for presenting prompts.

only if the verbal ones are ineffective. Dogs are not verbal, and in dog training many trainers often begin teaching a new skill with physical prompts (such as guiding the dog with a leash). Some trainers advocate a hands-off approach to training and believe that all behaviors can be shaped with no physical prompts. But, in general, providing some level of physical prompt is a much faster way to teach new skills.

Most of the top-rated trainers in all areas of canine competition are highly skilled at using prompts and fading. Prompting, fading and transferring stimulus control are the procedures that will develop a dog with behavior you can count on.

Chapter 13

chaining

··

Building behavior sequences

We thought we'd seen it all. We've seen police dogs scaling high walls and jumping through windows. We've seen service dogs pushing elevator buttons and passing money to bank tellers. We've seen movie dogs trained to smile and wave goodbye, and we've seen tracking dogs finding objects dropped in swiftly moving water.

But when we saw this, we were astounded. A Border Collie was doing the Macarena! One thousand experienced dog trainers were spellbound, and a Border Collie was on her hind legs doing a South American dance.

The Border Collie was Pepper, owned and trained by Sandra Davis of El Paso, Texas. Davis is an expert dog trainer and a nationally recognized member of the Pup-Peroni Canine Freestyle team. Canine freestyle is a new sport where dance routines for handlers and dogs are choreographed to music. In competition, handlers dance to three-minute routines that are judged in several categories. The Heinz Pup-Peroni Canine Freestylers, organized by Patie Ventre of New York, have been invited to perform at dog events and family pet expos all over the country. They are top crowd pleasers each and every time.

What makes Pepper's Macarena so spectacular? Chaining. Pepper doesn't just do one amazing movement or behavior; each exciting, unbelievable behavior leads immediately to the next. She has

> **Chaining** means combining behaviors in a planned sequence.

sequences of spinning, twirling, going through her owner's legs forward and backward, jumping and walking on her hind legs with her front legs stretched out in front of her in the Border Collie version of saucy Latin style.

Chaining can be used to teach elaborate sequences of behaviors. Sandra Davis, a Heinz Pup-Peroni Canine Freestyler, taught her Border Collie Pepper to do the Macarena.

The behaviors in a chaining sequence are related, and each one cues the next behavior. Ultimately, you reinforce only the last behavior in the behavioral chain.

CHAINS: FORWARD AND BACKWARD

There are two types of chaining: forward and backward. *Forward chaining* starts with the first response in the chain and progresses to the last response.

For example, if you wanted to teach your dog to pick up a toy and put it in the toy box, the steps would be:

1. Go to the toy.
2. Pick up the toy.
3. Take the toy to the box.
4. Drop the toy in the box.

Backward Chaining

Symbols for Explaining Backward Chaining

S^D = The cue, "drop it"

R = The response, dropping the toy

S^{R+} = The primary reinforcer, treats

Step 1. $S^D \rightarrow R_1 \rightarrow S^{R+}$

"Drop it"   Drops toy in box   Treat is given

Holly is standing over the toy box with the toy in her mouth. She is given the cue "drop it." Holly emits the response (drops the toy) and is immediately given the treat. This is done several times.

Step 2. $S^D \rightarrow R_2 \rightarrow R_1 \rightarrow S^{R+}$

Trainer gestures toward toy box and says "drop it"   Holly walks to toy box   Drops toy in box   Treat is given

Holly is two feet from the toy box with the toy in her mouth. Trainer gestures toward toy box. Holly goes to box, drops toy in box and immediately receives a treat. This is done several times.

Step 3. $S^D \rightarrow R_3 \rightarrow R_2 \rightarrow R_1 \rightarrow S^{R+}$

"Pick it up" and gesture toward toy   Picks up toy   Walks to toy box   Drops toy in box

Holly is two feet away from the toy box with the toy at her feet. The trainer says "pick it up" and gestures toward the toy box. Holly picks up the toy, takes it to the toy box, drops it and immediately receives a treat. This is done several times.

Step 4. $S^D \rightarrow R_4 \rightarrow R_3 \rightarrow R_2 \rightarrow R_1 \rightarrow S^{R+}$

"Pick it up" and gesture toward the toy   Goes to toy   Picks up toy   Walks to toy box   Drops toy in box

Holly is two feet from the toy. The trainer says "pick it up" and gestures toward the toy box. Holly goes to the toy, picks up the toy, takes it to the toy box, drops it and immediately receives a treat. This is done several times.

In forward chaining, the dog would be taught to do the first step of the chain first (go to the toy), then the second step and so on. In the last step of the forward chain, the dog would drop the toy into the box.

Backward chaining starts with the last response in the chain and moves backward to the first response. With the toy box example, you'd start by teaching the dog to drop a toy into the box. The last skill trained would be the first step of the chain, where the dog goes and picks up the toy.

CHAINING AS TRAINING

Chaining is one of the most commonly used procedures in advanced dog training. In beginning training, dogs are taught simple, single behaviors such as sit, come and down. In the more advanced, practical applications of dog training, the behavioral chains can become complex.

> The procedure of breaking a task into small steps to facilitate training is called **task analysis**. A task analysis identifies the stimulus and response for each step of the chain.

For example, service dogs that are trained to assist people with physical disabilities can go to the refrigerator, grab a towel tied on the refrigerator door, open the door, reach inside, pick up an item, bring it to the owner, return to the refrigerator and close the door. Chaining is the method used to tie this long string of skills together. Chaining moves a dog from a simple set of behaviors to a repertoire of complex tasks.

Things to Remember About Chaining

1. A task analysis is used to identify individual parts of the chain that are simple and can easily be learned by the dog.
2. Each skill in the chain is first taught individually.
3. The units must be taught in a logical sequence, and you must decide whether to use forward or backward chaining.
4. Reinforcers are gradually eliminated for every step of the chain (this is called *thinning*).
5. When the dog has learned the whole chain, reinforcement should be provided only at the end of the chain.

6. Reinforcement should eventually be delivered on an intermittent schedule. This will ensure that the dog will maintain the behavior over time.

7. You should determine that chaining is the appropriate technique for teaching new skills.

8. Dogs should have all the necessary physical and prerequisite skills needed for learning specific complex tasks.

9. Prompts and fading are important parts of any chaining procedure because the ultimate goal is to fade assistance.

Chapter 14

using conditioned reinforcement

....

Click here for more options

What do "Good job," "You look *mah*-velous," and "Congratulations, here is your Canine Good Citizen certificate" have in common? All are conditioned reinforcers. As you can see, conditioned reinforcers are important to both people and animals.

In Chapter 3 we outlined the different types of reinforcers and the various reinforcement schedules, and discussed how important it is that reinforcers have meaning for the animal being trained. Things like food and play are positive and meaningful to most animals, and are primary reinforcers. But other things, such as praise or a specific gesture or sound, can become reinforcers if the animal is conditioned to recognize them as such.

Praise is the most commonly used conditioned reinforcer. It is often used inconsistently and in conjunction with training methods that range from totally positive to strong, aversive punishers.

One form of conditioned reinforcement that has commanded a great deal of attention in recent years is the clicker. Clickers were being used as conditioned reinforcers by Marian and Keller Breland in the 1940s. Now, some 50 years later, there is a clicker training newsletter, and clicker seminars are taught throughout the country. There are clicker books, clicker videotapes, clicker jewelry and other gadgets, as well as printed materials related to using clickers with dogs, birds, cats, horses and llamas.

In the 1980s, animal trainer and author Karen Pryor gave the keynote speech at the Association for Behavior Analysis conference. She told behavioral scientists about animal training, and she began to teach animal trainers about the science of behavior. (You'll find more about Pryor in Chapter 2.)

Keeping up with the constant push to have a new twist on a popular idea, some trainers and seminar leaders are offering their unique take on clicker training. Some propose using whistles instead of clickers, although the functional purpose is the same.

Whether a clicker or a whistle is used, many trainers are extremely excited about clicker training. After years of learning dog training techniques that are compulsive and sometimes aversive for both the dog and the trainer, clicker training offers a positive way to teach new skills.

HOW CLICKER TRAINING WORKS

In clicker training, as in all conditioned reinforcement training, a reinforcer is paired with a neutral stimulus, and the neutral stimulus eventually becomes a conditioned reinforcer.

> In clicker training, the clicker is the neutral stimulus that becomes a conditioned reinforcer.

You start by using a primary reinforcer (most often a food treat). The treat is held in one hand, the clicker in the other. To begin, the treat is shown to the dog. As the dog reaches for the treat, you click the clicker, then give the dog the treat. After a few pairings, the dog learns that the clicking sound is followed by the treat. The click is now a conditioned reinforcer.

Once the dog makes the connection, the clicker (or whistle, or whatever stimulus you've selected) can be used as a reinforcer to teach a basic skill. For example, to teach a puppy to sit, hold the treat in one hand and the clicker in the other. The hand with the treat is moved over the dog's head and toward its back. (This is the lure method first described by Ian Dunbar. When food lures are used, dogs will follow the trainer's hand to get the food, and can be guided into a sit or down.) As soon as the dog starts to sit, click and follow up immediately with the treat. Eventually, the food lure is faded and the word "sit" is added as the cue for sitting. The click, however, remains as the conditioned reinforcer.

TARGET STICKS: FOLLOW THAT STICK!

Another procedure animal trainers use in operant conditioning is *targeting*. In targeting, the animal is taught to follow a moving target in order to get reinforced.

Dolphin trainers at Epcot Center in Florida have taught seals and sea lions to target their fists. When the animals are not in the water and the trainers want them to move, they present their hand in a fist and begin walking. The seals and sea lions follow along with such consistency they could earn excellent competitive dog obedience scores for heeling!

Many of the dog trainers who are using clickers are also using target sticks. Target sticks can be helpful in training a dog to jump over hurdles, to move away from its owner or to climb on agility equipment.

Targeting gives the trainer stimulus control for particular behaviors.

WHY USE CLICKER TRAINING?

Clicker training, which basically makes use of conditioned reinforcement, provides one more tool for teaching a dog new skills. Clicker trainers who swear by the method prefer the totally positive aspect of the training. Clicker training makes dog owners feel like trainers, and there is a lot to be said for how people perform when they feel empowered and have some special skills.

Clicker training is certainly a humane training method, and it does not result in abuse. It can be used to teach puppies to learn in a fun, positive way. For trainers who tend to be overly verbal, clicker training takes all the chatter out of training, helping the dog to concentrate on the task at hand.

Clicker training can be extremely useful in working with dogs that have been abused, are phobic, or that, for other reasons, do not like handling. Clickers can be used initially with these fearful dogs to teach them that good things come from their owner.

Clicker trainers have formed a happy, helpful clicker clique (no pun intended), and for some people the camaraderie afforded by participating in such a group provides a source of motivation. The strong network of clicker trainers offers a forum for discussion and education and a place where these trainers can work together to creatively solve learning problems. In fact, the clicker colleagues provide conditioned reinforcement to each other.

WHY NOT USE CLICKER TRAINING

The reasons why trainers might choose not to use clicker training are varied. Some are traditional by nature and prefer the standard methods of training because that is how they were taught. Some instructors believe traditional methods are more straight-forward and better lend themselves to the large group classes that most trainers offer.

Even young puppies such as this 12-week-old Bernese Mountain Dog can learn new skills with clicker training. This pup has learned to shake and is eager to play the clicker game. (courtesy of Anya Wittenborg)

Clicker training can easily teach simple behaviors such as sit, down or follow a target stick, but some trainers cannot figure out how to use the method to teach complex chains of behavior or more advanced skills. Clickers are also somewhat contrived and unnatural. The ultimate goal of many owners is a dog that will work for praise and petting, and they would just as soon bypass any additional phase of training, such as conditioning a clicker as a secondary reinforcer.

Some people are uncoordinated or awkward. They (or their obedience instructors) think it takes all their concentration just to manage a dog on a leash. Adding a clicker in one hand and food in the other is more than they can deal with. This is a bigger issue than you might think: Timing is extremely important in clicker training. Trainers who use clickers incorrectly and make reinforcement errors sometimes shape strange behaviors and quickly abandon the clicker.

To use clickers for functional training (and not just demonstrations), trainers must be skilled at using fading and schedules of reinforcement. We observed one trainer at a dog event who had missed the whole point. She used her clicker and delivered treats on a schedule that looked something like, "click, treat, treat, treat, click, click, click, treat, click, treat, click, click." The dog was having a very hard time figuring out what it was supposed to do!

THE LAST WORD
ON CONDITIONED REINFORCEMENT

Having a dog that will work for conditioned reinforcement is the ultimate goal of training. Currently, the most systematic application of conditioned reinforcement used with dogs is clicker training. Clicker training is an excellent method for shaping new behaviors or improving proficiency. However, it is not the best choice to reinforce skills the dog has already learned. When the dog has acquired the desired behavior, trainers are probably better off moving to less intrusive forms of conditioned reinforcement, such as praise and petting.

Some people think clicker training is an all-or-nothing methodology, like converting to a new religion. "Well, I'd just like for those clicker people to show me how to get a Utility title on a dog using a clicker," they say. Oops! They've missed the point. Clicker training, or more accurately, the use of conditioned reinforcement, is just one more method that any well-educated, well-rounded trainer can use when training a dog. In training dogs, sometimes the most appropriate method will involve fading. Sometimes shaping should be used. Clicker training simply adds to the trainer's arsenal yet one more technique that can be used to provide dogs with conditioned reinforcement.

Because it requires precise timing and well-planned reinforcement schedules, clicker training requires adequate instruction or a person who can translate the instructions in a book and on a video into competent trainer behavior.

Part Five

decreasing behaviors: dealing with canine delinquents

....

Training is not always about teaching dogs new skills. Sometimes what you really want to teach them is to decrease or stop a behavior. The operant techniques of extinction, differential reinforcement, antecedent control and punishment are combined with positive reinforcement of desired behaviors to decrease or eliminate problem behavior.

Chapter 15

extinction in action

Don't just do something, stand there

We talked about extinction in Chapter 4, but to refresh your memory, it's a technique that can be used to reduce or eliminate inappropriate behaviors that are not harmful to the individual or others. Extinction is one of the first

approaches trainers can use to address a behavior problem. It can be a good alternative to punishment when you are trying to eliminate unwanted behaviors.

Extinction is withholding a reinforcer that maintains a behavior.

Things to Remember About Using Extinction

When you're trying to decide whether extinction is the best approach to take in dealing with a problem, there are some points to keep in mind:

1. You must determine whether it is safe to use extinction. Never ignore dangerous or harmful behaviors such as aggression or self-injury.

2. You must identify what is reinforcing the problem behavior. What is maintaining this behavior? Attention? Something in the dog's environment?

3. The reinforcer must be withheld after each and every instance of the problem behavior.

4. You *must* reinforce alternative behaviors when using extinction. This is a critical part of using extinction. Otherwise, the problem behavior can be replaced with behaviors that are even worse.

5. If other people are working with the dog, make sure they will also use extinction, so there is consistency in the training.

6. If there is an extinction burst (where the behavior gets worse), can you tolerate it and see the training through?

7. You must work to generalize the effects of extinction to new, appropriate behaviors over time and under a variety of conditions.

8. Can you handle any possible side effects of extinction, such as aggression, a dog that suddenly becomes pushy for attention, emotional responses or agitation?

9. Extinction can be used effectively only when the trainer has control of the reinforcers. For example, ignoring a barking dog will not solve the problem if the dog is barking at squirrels.

10. All of the physical and biological needs of the animal must be met before starting extinction. For example, it would not be appropriate to put a puppy in a crate and ignore its whining if it had not been taken out for several hours.

CASE STUDY: A WHINING WELSH

Sarge was a well-socialized Welsh Springer Spaniel puppy whose owners (the authors of this book) decided the time had come for him to be crate trained. The first time Sarge was put in a crate, he behaved like a dog possessed. He yelped, barked, whined, howled like a Husky and bayed like a Beagle. He alternated between sounding lonely, miserable and pitiful and sounding downright angry. At the risk of sounding anthropomorphic, we'd say that Sarge was probably certain he'd been sold to the wrong home.

We chose extinction to deal with Sarge's behavior. Data collection began one evening at 11:20 P.M. Sarge was given the verbal cue, "Get in your crate." His whining was ignored, and as can be seen from the graph, within a few sessions the puppy was almost completely crate trained.

To speed up Sarge's progress, several short crate training sessions were held each day. When Sarge was quiet in the crate for 15 minutes, the door was opened and he was taken outside to play—reinforcement for good behavior.

Extinction of Whining

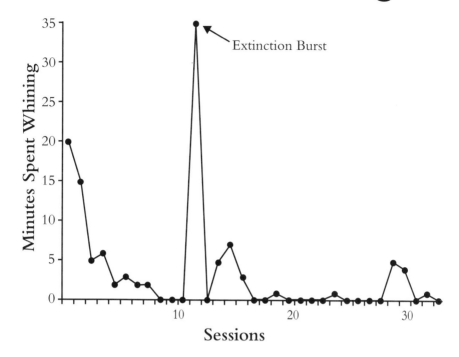

After making good progress in the crate, during the 12th daytime practice session Sarge yelped, barked and carried on like the world was ending for 34 minutes, nonstop. This was the classic extinction burst, in which the frequency and the rate of the behavior increase before the final decline. We toughed it out, and, as the graph shows, Sarge's whining problem was eventually eliminated.

THE LAST WORD ON EXTINCTION

Unaware of the extinction burst phenomenon, some dog owners experience the burst of unwanted behavior and say, "Forget it, this isn't working." Don't be one of them! Extinction *does* work when used properly.

It's also worth repeating that the dog must be taught appropriate behaviors and given reinforcement for those behaviors (we'll explain how to do this in Chapter 16). In Sarge's case, the appropriate behavior was to sit quietly in the crate. Play sessions reinforced that behavior.

If appropriate behaviors are not reinforced, the problem behavior can be replaced with behaviors that are even worse. Sarge may have switched from whining to self-mutilation, for instance, if we had not reinforced calm, quiet behavior.

Chapter 16

differential reinforcement

More of this, less of that

Dogs are great: They look at us as if we're gods, and then make us realize that we are mere mortals when we try to train them. Often, they don't make training easy. While we are busy trying to teach a new skill, we suddenly realize the dog has added some weird and very much unwanted behavior to the training session. We then find ourselves trying to increase one behavior while decreasing another.

There's an old joke that some people can't walk and chew gum at the same time. Simultaneous walking and chewing may not be a prerequisite for being a top-notch dog trainer, but having the knack for doing two things at once is.

> **Differential reinforcement** combines extinction and reinforcement to decrease the probability of an undesirable behavior while increasing the frequency of a desirable behavior.

You'll recall from our discussions of extinction that simply ignoring an undesired behavior is not sufficient. At the same time the inappropriate behavior is not being reinforced, it is important to reinforce a desirable behavior. This process is called *differential reinforcement*.

HOW IS DIFFERENTIAL REINFORCEMENT USED?

1. Identify the target behaviors: Which one will be reduced? Which one will be increased?
2. Choose the reinforcer.
3. Begin an extinction program for the undesirable behavior.
4. Reinforce the desirable behavior—immediately and consistently.
5. Have an ongoing evaluation of the results. If the plan is not working, something went wrong. If it is working, generalize the behavior to other settings.

VARIATIONS ON THE DIFFERENTIAL REINFORCEMENT THEME

Differential reinforcement can be used in several ways. Each variation works better in certain kinds of situations and with certain dogs. And, like all scientific terms, each variation has its own shorthand name. The various forms of differential reinforcement go by the letters DRI, DRA, DRL and DRO. The DR always stands for differential reinforcement, but let's look at what the rest of this alphabet soup means.

DRI

DRI is differential reinforcement of *incompatible* behaviors—reinforcing a behavior that is incompatible with the behavior you're trying to eliminate. In other words, if a dog is doing one thing, it can't do the other.

For example, dogs that jump on strangers can be taught to sit to greet people. Sitting is reinforced, and is incompatible with jumping up—a dog can't sit and jump up at the same time. Jumping on strangers decreases, but more important the dog has acquired a new skill that is an acceptable way of greeting people.

One way to reduce the frequency of an undesirable behavior is to reinforce a behavior that is incompatible with it. This is **differential reinforcement of incompatible behaviors**.

With dogs that dig excessively, one recommended treatment is providing them with an acceptable place in the yard for digging. This is also a form of differential reinforcement of incompatible behaviors. Digging in the doggy digging place is incompatible with digging in the bed of prize day lilies.

Differential reinforcement can be used to teach dogs that like digging to excavate only in their own special place.

DRA

In differential reinforcement of incompatible behaviors, you choose an incompatible response and systematically reinforce it. But sometimes it is not practical to come up with an incompatible behavior. That's where *DRA*, differential reinforcement of *alternative* behaviors, comes in. With differential reinforcement of alternative behaviors, the animal (or person) is reinforced for engaging in a better alternative to the undesirable behavior— although the alternative behavior may not always be incompatible with the undesirable behavior.

Differential reinforcement of alternative behaviors teaches a dog that acceptable behaviors result in rewards, while undesirable behaviors do not.

For example, a hyper puppy that barks with excitement all the time might be trained to do some basic obedience tasks. As the puppy learns the tasks, it earns reinforcement by following a food lure to sit, lie down and stand, and eventually the barking stops. Of course a puppy can sit and bark at the same time, but it has learned that the alternative behaviors are the ones that get the rewards. In this case, timing the food reinforcer is crucial, so the dog does not get rewarded when it is barking.

DRL

DRL, differential reinforcement of *low-rate* behaviors, is used when some level of a behavior is acceptable, but less is better. In this case, the behavior is reinforced only when it occurs infrequently.

With **differential reinforcement of low-rate behaviors**, trainers reinforce behaviors only if they occur less often than a specific number of times in a given period.

Differential reinforcement of low-rate behaviors can be used to slow down dogs that are performing a task too rapidly. For example, a service dog that is supposed to pick up objects and bring them to its owner might be trained to fetch, wait, fetch, wait, in order to give the person with a physical disability the time needed to respond. Fetching might be rewarded only when it occurs once a minute.

DRO

DRO, differential reinforcement of *other* behaviors, involves reinforcing a desirable behavior when an undesirable behavior does not occur for a certain amount of time. In school settings, differential reinforcement of other behaviors is commonly used to address disruption in the classroom. For example, the teacher might set a timer, and for every five minutes the children are not disruptive, they earn one minute of free time.

Differential reinforcement of other behaviors reinforces the absence of an undesirable behavior for a specified period of time.

With dogs, differential reinforcement of other behaviors can be used to address problems such as whining when the dog is in a crate. If the crated dog does not whine for, say, 15 minutes, it is taken out, hugged, praised and given a play session. If the dog whines, the 15-minute clock is reset. The case of Sarge, described in Chapter 15, is a good example of how this works.

Chapter 17

antecedent control

....

An ounce of prevention

In Chapter 6 on stimulus control we talked about how controlling the *antecedent stimulus* (the stimulus that comes before a behavior) can affect the behavioral outcome. Put another way, if you carefully analyze a dog's behavior problem, it may be possible to solve the problem by making simple changes in the dog's environment.

Understanding what is causing the problem behavior is the tricky part. Once you do, antecedent control is easy. This technique is especially nice because it may often be used in place of punishment—and nobody enjoys punishing their dog.

As with just about every concept in operant conditioning, antecedent control can be broken down into several types. In this case, there are six of them.

> **Antecedent control** involves controlling the environment so that a problem behavior will not occur.

REMOVE A CUE FOR MISBEHAVIOR

One antecedent control procedure is simply removing the cue for a behavior problem. Sparky is a terrier-spaniel mix who goes to work every day with his owner. Sparky is causing problems because he sits at the floor-length window in the office and barks at anything outside that moves.

The owner could choose to yell at Sparky or smack him for barking; that would be punishment. Antecedent control solutions involve removing the cues for barking. The owner could cover the window or move Sparky's bed to the other side of the office.

ADD A CUE FOR BEING GOOD

In Sparky's case, his owner could also provide new cues for a desirable behavior—being quiet in the office. One possibility is teaching Sparky the commands "bark" and "quiet." He could be cued to bark at appropriate times (outside, at home or occasionally to say hello to someone in the office) and to be quiet most of the time. Another possibility is to put alternative behaviors for barking on cue, such as "play with your toy," "chew your bone" or "get in your bed." You'll notice this solution overlaps with differential reinforcement of alternative behaviors.

ADD AN ESTABLISHING OPERATION
FOR BEING GOOD

Another antecedent control strategy for decreasing a problem behavior is to create an establishing operation that will make a desirable behavior more likely to occur (we discussed establishing operations in Chapter 3).

Ajax is an Akita that destroyed his owner's possessions regularly when he was left alone uncrated during the day. Ajax was crate trained, and his owner decided to use the crate. In the morning, Ajax was put in the crate while the owner got ready for work. After a few days, Ajax started running to the far corners of the yard to avoid coming in the house and going in the crate.

Ajax's owner decided going into the crate had to be a more reinforcing experience. He got up one hour earlier and took Ajax for a walk around the neighborhood. When he returned to the yard, he and Ajax had a short, active play session before he went in to get ready for work. By then, Ajax was tired out and was more willing to come in and get into his crate. In this case, the walk and play session was the establishing operation.

REMOVE AN ESTABLISHING OPERATION
FOR MISBEHAVIOR

You probably remember from Chapter 3 that when you remove the establishing operation for a reinforcing event, its effectiveness as a reinforcer is diminished. Bruiser was a Doberman Pinscher that lived with an older couple. He was a sociable dog and loved attention. The guests who came to visit most often were the couple's adult children, all of whom liked dogs. When these family members came to visit, Bruiser would jump up and get very excited. He was allowed to visit momentarily, and then his embarrassed owners would drag him to the guest room and shut the door.

The solution was to tell all family visitors to sit down as soon as they arrived, so the dog could not jump on them. They were also instructed to give Bruiser plenty of attention throughout the visit because, in his case, lack of attention was the establishing operation. When they went to the kitchen, they had him come along. When they went to sit on the patio, Bruiser went too. The visitors removed the establishing operation, thus making the dog less likely to engage in his hyper, out-of-control behaviors to get attention.

DECREASE THE RESPONSE EFFORT FOR GOOD BEHAVIOR

The last two ways of using antecedent control to decrease behaviors involve manipulating the response effort required for the dog to engage in behaviors. Response effort manipulations are more easily done with humans than with dogs, but there are some canine applications.

As you might expect, decreasing the effort required for the dog to engage in a desired behavior will increase the likelihood the behavior will occur. In other words, make it easier to be good and the dog is more likely to be good.

Response effort is the effort the dog must make in order to engage in a behavior.

Some owners who want their dog to play with toys or chew a rawhide bone will keep the toys in a box or out of view from company—perhaps in the kitchen or on a porch. This means the dog has to leave the room where the family is to get a chew toy, or it has to beg for the toy box to be opened. That's a lot of effort. If the toys are easily accessible in the main living area, using them requires much less effort, and the dog may be more likely to do so.

When dogs get older, sometimes they develop house-training problems. Oftentimes, walking down the steps to get outside is just too much trouble for an older dog. These dogs will wet their bedding rather than get up to go outside. Ramps to replace the steps and other prosthetic devices can decrease the response effort required to go outside, and thus make the desired behavior more likely to occur.

INCREASE THE RESPONSE EFFORT
FOR PROBLEM BEHAVIOR

Increasing the effort required for the dog to engage in a problem behavior can result in the decrease of that behavior. For example, the owner of three Schipperkes wanted the dogs to use a dog door to let themselves into the backyard. The dogs started using the door to run in and out all the time, acting as if the activity itself was entertaining. But this constant coming and going, with the dog door always flapping, was annoying. The owner adjusted the door so it required more force to enter and exit. The result of increasing the response effort was that the dogs stopped running in and out all the time.

Adjusting the door took care of the immediate problem, but ideally the whole situation would be analyzed to solve this or any other behavior problem. Why were the dogs running in and out? Were they bored? Training, and appropriate activities with the owner, should also have been provided.

While increasing the response effort to decrease problem behavior may be a good strategy for humans (such as making it harder for a smoker to get cigarettes), it is not appropriate with dogs. We don't want to simply make it harder for dogs to engage in problem behaviors; we want to analyze the problem, eliminate the behavior and replace it with new, adaptive skills.

Chapter 18

using punishment

A question of ethics

Sometimes we are magnificent as trainers of dogs and humans, and other times our brilliant ideas don't turn out exactly as we planned.

In his book *The Sin of Wages,* William Abernathy, an internationally recognized business consultant, tells a story about trying to demonstrate the difference between positive and negative reinforcement. Abernathy was teaching a class on performance management to prison guards, who had a tendency to use plenty of negative reinforcement and punishment. To demonstrate the benefits of positive reinforcement, Abernathy took two rats and two Skinner boxes to the prison. (A Skinner box is a box designed to teach an animal to press a bar. It can be set up to offer either positive or negative reinforcement.) He used shaping to teach the first rat to press a bar in the box to receive positive reinforcement—a food pellet. Exactly as expected, the rat was pressing the bar for food in about 30 minutes.

The second rat was put in a Skinner box that was set to deliver mild shocks. To avoid the shock, the rat was negatively reinforced for bar pressing—pressing the bar would prevent future shocks. Usually, teaching the rat to press the bar takes much longer with negative reinforcement than with positive reinforcement. The rat is so busy trying to escape the shock, it doesn't engage in the desired responses at first.

On this particular day, however, something very strange happened in the negative reinforcement demonstration. Somehow, as soon as the shock came on, the rat jumped up to avoid the shock and landed directly on the bar, turning off the current. To Abernathy's dismay, the guards witnessed a freak accident where negative reinforcement worked much faster than positive reinforcement, perhaps strengthening their belief in management through intimidation and punishment.

Abernathy told everyone to take a break. During the break, one of the guards picked up the rat that had received the positive reinforcement and began to play with it. A second guard saw this and decided to play with the negatively reinforced rat. When he picked it up, the rat immediately bit his finger. He began to swing the rat around, but it would not let go. Finally, after the rat had been separated from the guard's bloody finger, one guard summarized what he had learned in the day's lesson. "Well," he said, "you can get someone to do what you want through negative reinforcement; you just don't want to be around them!"

This is a true story, and it gives dog trainers something to think about. When you train a dog that associates you with positive reinforcement, the dog is usually happy and eager to come to you. When you use a great deal of punishment in your training, the dog will not be as eager to work with you. Smart dog!

Remember that punishment is a continuum, and the levels of punishment vary from mild to highly aversive. Mild forms of punishment include withdrawing attention (time out) and verbal reprimands such as "No!" or "Ahh!" Physical punishers range from mild snap-release leash corrections to shock collars.

SHOCK TREATMENT

Because an electric shock is so aversive, shock is perhaps the most controversial form of punishment in dog training. Shock collars are used by some hunting dog and Schutzhund trainers because the collars provide a way of controlling the dog when it is working at a distance.

Electronic fencing also involves the use of shock as a punisher. A wire is buried around the perimeter of the yard, and the dog is fitted with a special collar that delivers a shock when it crosses the perimeter. There are also shock mats designed to prevent animals from getting on the furniture, and shock collars that are activated when a dog barks.

Shock collars have settings that permit different levels of shock. Milder levels are supposedly used for training, and more intense levels are used to deliver punishment. Shock collars are currently used by some expert trainers, and they are sold to novice dog owners who don't have a clue how shock can affect their dogs. We've seen many dogs wearing shock collars that are jumpy, nervous and quick to bite if touched when they didn't expect it. Obviously, this is not the kind of behavior their owners were trying to elicit.

GUIDELINES FOR USING PUNISHMENT

With any form of punishment, you need to consider some very important issues. If punishment is to be used, you must attempt to reduce any negative side effects by providing a reinforcement schedule that is rich in positive reinforcement for appropriate behaviors.

Then decide on the form and intensity of punishment. The least aversive method that will be effective should be used. If "No!" corrects the problem, it is not ethical to use anything more intense.

Try the punisher on yourself. Any trainer who considers using aversive punishers such as a shock collar should first try the shock on himself or herself in order to be aware of the level of physical discomfort the animal will experience.

Punishment should be delivered consistently, and immediately after the problem behavior. And any time punishment is used, the dog should be learning new replacement skills for the inappropriate behavior and should be receiving a rich schedule of positive reinforcement.

TOUGH QUESTIONS ABOUT PUNISHMENT

If trainers were asked to list some reasons for using punishment, one would be that punishment can be effective in decreasing behavior problems. Another might be that milder forms of punishment seem to be easier to use than positive reinforcement procedures. Finally, some trainers believe that for certain dogs with severe behavior problems, not using punishment would mean withholding a potentially successful treatment.

Most dog trainers will admit that they see a place for mild forms of punishment, such as withholding attention for misbehavior, verbal reprimands and leash corrections. The real controversy begins with more aversive punishers, such as smacking the dog under the chin and using pinch or shock collars.

The majority of trainers would not use intensive aversive procedures such as these for routine training or mild behavior problems. But at some point, once we get beyond the mild punishers, we have to make difficult ethical decisions. Would you shock a dog for getting into the garbage? We hope not. Would you shock a former racing Greyhound for chasing cats if you knew the dog would end up in a shelter if the cat chasing didn't stop? Would it make

Steps That Should Precede the Use of Aversive Punishers with Dogs

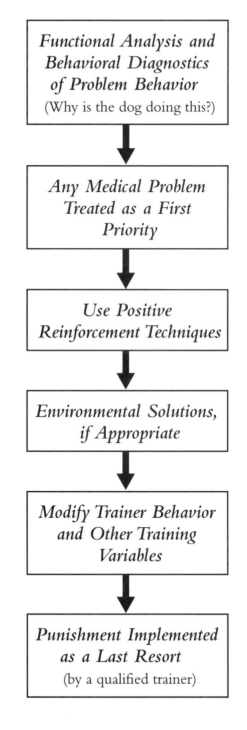

Functional Analysis and
Behavioral Diagnostics
of Problem Behavior
(Why is the dog doing this?)

↓

Any Medical Problem
Treated as a First
Priority

↓

Use Positive
Reinforcement Techniques

↓

Environmental Solutions,
if Appropriate

↓

Modify Trainer Behavior
and Other Training
Variables

↓

Punishment Implemented
as a Last Resort
(by a qualified trainer)

A CANINE BILL OF RIGHTS

1. Dogs have a right to a rich, stimulating environment.
2. Dogs have a right to time and attention from a caring owner.
3. Dogs have a right to effective training procedures; if behavior problems are to be addressed, a competent person must be involved.
4. Dogs have a right to ongoing veterinary care and a comprehensive assessment (functional analysis and behavioral diagnostics) for behavior problems.
5. Dogs have a right to an ongoing education and the chance to learn new skills.

We should treat the dogs we love the way we'd like to be treated.

a difference in your decision if you were told that to fix the problem behavior you would have to shock the dog for months? Would it make a difference if you were told that two or three mild shocks would fix the problem?

What about the dog living in the country that develops a fondness for
"herding" deer? Would you consider shock as a punishment if you believed
that the dog might accidentally be shot by a hunter?

Would you use aversive punishers to stop a behavior that could result in
injury to people or other animals? These are the kinds of questions dog
owners and trainers need to think about. The punishment controversy is not
as simple as all-or-nothing.

These are exciting times for dog trainers. The Association of Pet Dog
Trainers (APDT) is developing a Code of Ethics, and there is potential for
dog training to develop as a respected profession. In human psychology,
behavior analysis has seen tremendous growth as a profession in the last few
decades. Some states now certify behavior analysts, and dog trainers can
benefit from lessons learned in human behavioral treatment.

In developmental disabilities facilities in Florida, all staff are permitted
to use positive reinforcement with clients. The effective use of punishment
procedures, such as time out, requires more training, and only a certified
behavior analyst may implement the more aversive forms of punishment.
Even then, the punishment is approved, reviewed carefully and monitored
by qualified staff outside of the facility.

THE LAST WORD ON PUNISHMENT

Any decision to use punishment should be made *only* after trying positive
alternatives. The use of aversive punishment procedures can be justified only
if the problem behavior presents a threat to the dog's well-being or the safety
of other people or animals. Aversive punishers, such as shock, should *never* be
put in the hands of unskilled, novice dog owners. The bottom line when it
comes to ethics is that our dogs love us. We owe it to them to treat them the
same way we'd like to be treated.

epilogue

Since the 1960s, dog training has undergone a revolution, with the majority of dog owners and trainers moving toward a more positive, motivational philosophy of training. While most people once wanted a dog that would comply with requests because it was afraid to do otherwise, training has changed dramatically. Now, most people want a dog that will work because it wants to.

Operant conditioning provides an explanation of the basic principles underlying how this goal can be achieved. It offers effective training procedures and provides guidelines for how dogs and their owners can be trained more effectively.

Functional analysis and behavioral diagnostics are tools that can be used in conjunction with operant conditioning to analyze canine behavior problems in a way that results in humane solutions that do not involve blaming the dog.

Operant conditioning explains how dogs learn.

These are such exciting times for those of us who love dogs! We can all look forward to watching dog training transform itself from a haphazard, trial-and-error group of techniques to a field where sophisticated, educated trainers use the most modern teaching technologies possible.

When we understand the science related to how dogs learn, we can begin to weed out all the fads and fallacies floating around in dog training. For example, does feeding your dog only after you eat really make a dog more obedient? Maybe so, but not for the reasons you've probably heard. Some trainers who conceptualize a dog-owning family as a wolf pack believe making a dog wait to eat is part of a tightly controlled program that will teach the dog that its master is above it in the pack hierarchy. But what really happens when you feed your dog on a rigid schedule? You start giving clear instructions, applying consequences and reinforcing acceptable behavior. The change in the dog's overall behavior has nothing to do with an ethological, cognitive canine thought such as, "Oh, she really put me in my place. I'm not as important as I thought." The change can easily be explained in terms of the contingencies of reinforcement.

Operant behaviors are controlled by consequences, and in dog training almost all of those consequences are mediated by the trainer. But the beauty of using operant procedures is that the learning and shaping process goes both ways. Owners and trainers who use positive reinforcement to shape their dogs will soon find that the dogs are shaping them. Nothing is more fun than being approached by a dog who gives you that canine look and body language that says, "Let's go! It's time for training!"

references

Chapter 1

Allyon, T., and J. Michael.(1959). "The psychiatric nurse as a behavioral engineer." *Journal of the Experimental Analysis of Behavior,* 2:323–334.

Association for Behavior Analysis. Western Michigan University, 213 West Hall, Kalamazoo, MI 49008-5052. (616) 387-8342. (For information on SEAB, JEAB, ABA, JABA and the ABA Animal Trainer's Forum.)

Bailey, B., and M. B. Bailey. (1996). *Patient Like the Chipmunks.* Eclectic Science Productions.

Burch, M. (1996). *The Border Collie: An Owner's Guide to a Happy, Healthy Pet.* New York: Howell Book House.

Joncich, G. (1968). *The Sane Positivist: A Biography of Edward L. Thorndike.* Middletown, Connecticut: Wesleyan University Press.

Keller, F. S., and W. N. Schoenfeld. (1950). *Principles of Psychology: A Systematic Text in the Science of Behavior.* New York: Appleton-Century-Crofts.

Michael, J. (1982). Distinguishing between discriminative and motivational functions of stimuli. *Journal of the Experimental Analysis of Behavior,* 37:149–155.

Schwartz, B., and H. Lacey. (1982). *Behaviorism, Science and Human Nature.* New York: W.W. Norton.

Skinner, B.F. (1938). *The Behavior of Organisms: An Experimental Analysis.* New York: Appleton-Century.

Skinner, B.F. (1951). "How to teach animals." *Scientific American.*

Chapter 2

American Kennel Club. (1985). *The American Kennel Club: 1884–1984.* New York: Howell Book House.

American Kennel Club. (1998). *The Complete Dog Book*. 19th ed. rev. New York: Howell Book House.

Animal Behavior Consultant Newsletter. c/o Dr. John Wright, Mercer University, Department of Psychology, 1400 Coleman Ave., Macon, GA 31207-0001.

Animal Behavior Society. c/o Dr. John Wright. Mercer University, Department of Psychology, 1400 Coleman Ave., Macon, GA 31207-0001.

Burch, M., and D. Pickel. (1990). "A toast to Most: A 1910 pioneer in animal training." *Journal of Applied Behavior Analysis,* 23(2):263–64.

Campbell, W. E. (1992). *Behavior Problems in Dogs*. Goleta, California: American Veterinary Publications.

Front & Finish. Bob Self, sr. ed. P.O. Box 333, Galesburg, IL 61402-0333.

Koehler, W. (1962). *The Koehler Method of Dog Training*. New York: Howell Book House.

Miltenberger, R. (1997). *Behavior Modification: Principles and Practices*. Pacific Grove, California: Brooks/Cole Publishing .

Most, C. (1954). *Training Dogs: A Manual*. Great Britain: The Anchor Press.

Offlead: The Dog Training Instructors Magazine. Don Arner, ed. 204 Lewis Street, Canastota, NY 13032.

Pearsall, M., and C. Leedham. (1958). *Dog Obedience Training*. New York: Charles Scribner's Sons.

Pet Behavior Newsletter. William Campbell, ed. P.O. Box 1658, Grants Pass, OR 97528.

Pfaffenberger, C. (1963). *The New Knowledge of Dog Behavior*. New York: Howell Book House.

Pryor, K. (1985). *Don't Shoot the Dog! The New Art of Teaching and Training*. New York: Bantam Books.

Saunders, B. (1954). *The Complete Book of Dog Obedience*. New York: Howell Book House.

Scott, J. P., and J. Fuller. (1965). *Genetics and the Social Behavior of the Dog*. Chicago: University of Chicago Press.

Weber, J. (1939). *The Dog in Training*. New York: Whittlesey House.

Chapter 3

Amsel, A., and M. Stanton. (1980). "Ontogeny and phylogeny of paradoxical reward effects." *Advances in the Study of Animal Behavior,* ed. J.S. Rosenblatt, R.A. Hinde, C. Beer, and M.C. Busnel. New York: Academic Press.

Ayllon, T., and N. H. Azrin. (1968). "Reinforcer sampling: A technique for increasing the behavior of mental patients." *Journal of Applied Behavior Analysis,* 1:13–20.

Chance, P. (1998). *First Course in Applied Behavior Analysis.* Pacific Grove, California: Brooks/Cole Publishing.

Cooper, J., T. Heron, and W. Heward. (1987). *Applied Behavior Analysis.* Columbus, Ohio: Merrill Publishing.

Crespi, L. P. (1942). "Quantitative variation in incentive performance in the white rat." *The American Journal of Psychology,* 40:467–517.

Flaherty, C. (1985). *Animal Learning and Cognition.* New York: McGraw-Hill.

Flaherty, C. (1996). *Incentive Relativity.* New York: Cambridge University Press.

Kazdin, A. (1994). *Behavior Modification in Applied Settings.* Pacific Grove, California: Brooks/Cole Publishing.

Martin, G., and J. Pear. (1996). *Behavior Modification: What It Is and How to Do It.* Upper Saddle River, New Jersey: Prentice Hall.

Michael, J. (1982). "Distinguishing between discriminative and motivational functions of stimuli." *Journal of the Experimental Analysis of Behavior,* 37:149–155.

Pryor, K. (1995). *On Behavior.* North Bend, Washington: Sunshine Books.

Rashotte, M. E. (1979). "Reward training: Contrast effects." *Animal Learning: Survey and Analysis,* ed. M. E. Bitterman, V. M. LoLordo, J. B. Overmier, and M. E. Rashotte. New York: Plenum Press.

Rashotte, M. E. (1979). "Reward training: Extinction." *Animal Learning: Survey and Analysis,* ed. M. E. Bitterman, V. M. LoLordo, J. B. Overmier, and M. E. Rashotte. New York: Plenum Press.

Schwartz, B., and H. Lacey. (1982). *Behaviorism, Science, and Nature.* New York: W. W. Norton.

Chapter 4

Burch, M. (1996). *Volunteering With Your Pet: How to get involved in animal-assisted therapy with any kind of pet.* New York: Howell Book House.

Rashotte, M. E. (1979). "Reward training: Extinction." *Animal Learning: Survey and Analysis,* ed. M. E. Bitterman, V. M. LoLordo, J. B. Overmier, and M. E. Rashotte. New York: Plenum Press.

Skinner, B.F. (1938). *The Behavior of Organisms: An Experimental Analysis.* New York: Appleton-Century.

Chapter 5

Chance, P. (1998). *First Course in Applied Behavior Analysis.* Pacific Grove, California: Brooks/Cole Publishing.

Lindsay, S. (1997). "The use and abuse of punishment." *APDT Newsletter,* 4(6):1–16.

Martin, G., and J. Pear. (1996). *Behavior Modification: What It Is and How to Do It.* Upper Saddle River, New Jersey: Prentice Hall.

Miltenberger, R. (1997). *Behavior Modification: Principles and Procedures.* Pacific Grove, California: Brooks/Cole Publishing.

Van Houten, R. (1983). "Punishment: From the animal laboratory to the applied setting." *The Effects of Punishment on Human Behavior,* ed. S. Axelrod and J. Apsche, (13–44). New York: Academic Press.

Van Houten, R., and S. Axelrod, eds. (1993). *Behavior Analysis and Treatment.* New York: Plenum Press.

Van Houten, R., S. Axelrod, J. S. Bailey, J. E. Favell, R. M. Foxx, B. A. Iwata, and O. I. Lovaas. (1988). "The right to effective behavioral treatment." *Journal of Applied Behavior Analysis,* 21:381–84.

Chapter 6

Burch, M. R., and D. Pickel. (1991). "Behavior analysis goes to the dogs: Reduce dropout rates in obedience classes by incorporating communication, reinforcement, and feedback." *Dog World Magazine,* 76(6): 56–59.

Martin, G., and J. Pear. (1996). *Behavior Modification: What It Is and How to Do It.* Upper Saddle River, New Jersey: Prentice Hall.

Michael, J. (1982). "Distinguishing between discriminative and motivational functions of stimuli." *Journal of the Experimental Analysis of Behavior,* 37:149–155.

Miltenberger, R. (1997). *Behavior Modification: Principles and Procedures.* Pacific Grove, California: Brooks/Cole Publishing.

Skinner, B.F. (1969). *Contingencies of Reinforcement: A Theoretical Analysis.* New York: Appleton-Century-Crofts.

Stokes, T. F., and D. M. Baer. (1977). "An implicit technology of generalization." *Journal of Applied Behavior Analysis,* 10:349–67.

Chapter 7

Bitterman, M. E., V. M. LoLordo, J. B. Overmier, M. E. Rashotte, M.E., eds. (1979). *Animal learning: Survey and analysis.* New York: Plenum Press.

Catania, C. (1979). *Learning*. Englewood Cliffs, New Jersey: Prentice Hall.

Chance, P. (1998). *First Course in Applied Behavior Analysis*. Pacific Grove, California: Brooks/Cole Publishing.

Flaherty, C. (1985). *Animal Learning and Cognition*. New York: McGraw-Hill.

Holland, J.G., and B.F. Skinner. (1961). *The Analysis of Behavior: A Program for Self-Instruction*. New York: McGraw-Hill.

Jones, M. C. (1924). "A laboratory study of fear: The case of Peter." *Journal of Experimental Psychology*, 7:308–15.

Miltenberger, R. (1997). *Behavior Modification: Principles and Practices*. Pacific Grove, California: Brooks/Cole Publishing.

Pavlov, I. P. (1927). *Conditioned Reflexes*. Trans.(G.V. Anrep.) London: Oxford University Press.

Rescorla, R.A. (1967). "Inhibition of delay in Pavlovian fear conditioning." *Journal of Comparative and Physiological Psychology*, 64:114–20.

Rescorla, R.A., and A. R. Wagner. (1972). "A theory of Pavlovian conditioning: Variation of the effectiveness of reinforcement and nonreinforcement." *Classical Conditioning II: Current Research and Theory*, ed. A. H. Black and W. F. Prokasy. New York: Appleton-Century-Crofts.

Rescorla, R.A. (1973). "Effect of US habituation following conditioning." *Journal of Comparative and Physiological Psychology*, 82, 137–143.

Reynolds, G.S. (1968). *A Primer of Operant Conditioning*. Palo Alto, California: Scott, Foresman.

Wolpe, J. (1958). *Psychotherapy by Reciprocal Inhibition*. Stanford, California: Stanford University Press.

Chapter 8

Pyles, D. A. M., and J. S. Bailey. (1989). "Behavioral diagnostics." *Monographs of the American Association on Mental Retardation*, 12:85–106.

Pyles, D.A.M., & Bailey, J.S. (1990). "Diagnosing severe behavior problems." A. Repp & N. Singh (Eds.), *Perspectives on the Use of Nonaversive and Aversive Interventions for Persons with Developmental Disabilities*, ed. A. Repp and N. Singh, 381–401. Sycamore, Illinois: Sycamore Publishing.

Chapter 9

Burch, M. R. (1996). *The Border Collie: An Owner's Guide to a Happy, Healthy Pet*. New York: Howell Book House.

Foster, R., and M. Smith. (1995). *What's the Diagnosis? Understanding Your Dog's Health Problems*. New York: Howell Book House.

Chapter 10

Breland, K., and M. Breland. (1961). "The misbehavior of organisms."
   American Psychologist.
Burch, M. (1996). *Volunteering with Your Pet.* New York: Howell Book House.
Scott, J. P., and J. L. Fuller. (1965). *Genetics and the Social Behavior of the Dog.*
   Chicago, Illinois: University of Chicago Press.

Chapter 11

Chance, P. (1998). *First Course in Applied Behavior Analysis.* Pacific Grove,
   California: Brooks/Cole Publishing.
Martin, G., and J. Pear. (1996). *Behavior Modification: What It Is and How to
   Do It.* Upper Saddle River, New Jersey: Prentice Hall.

Chapter 12

Chance, P. (1998). First Course in Applied Behavior Analysis. Pacific Grove,
   California: Brooks/Cole Publishing.
Miltenberger, R. (1997). *Behavior Modification: Principles and Procedures.* Pacific
   Grove, California: Brooks/Cole Publishing.

Chapter 13

Davis, S. (1997). *Dancing With Your Dog: Getting the Rhythm.* Dancing Dogs
   Video, P.O. Box 3324, El Paso, TX 79923.
Martin, G. & Pear, J. (1996). *Behavior Modification: What It Is and How to Do
   It.* Upper Saddle River, New Jersey: Prentice Hall.
Pup-Peroni Canine Freestylers. For more information contact: Patie Ventre,
   P.O. Box 350122, Brooklyn, NY 11235. (718) 646-2686. email:
   pupfreesty@aol.com

Chapter 14

Bailey, B., and M. B. Bailey. (1996). *Patient Like the Chipmunks.* Eclectic
   Science Productions.
Pryor, K. (1998). *Clicker Magic! The Art of Clicker Training.* (Video). North
   Bend, WA: Sunshine Books.
Skinner, B.F. (1938). *The Behavior of Organisms: An Experimental Analysis.*
   New York: Appleton-Century.

Chapter 15

Burch, M. (1990). The extinction of whining during crate training. *Off-Lead Dog Training,* 21(9):18–20.

Chance, P. (1998). *First Course in Applied Behavior Analysis.* Pacific Grove, California: Brooks/Cole Publishing.

Chapter 16

Cooper, J., T. Heron, W. Heward. (1987). *Applied Behavior Analysis.* Columbus, Ohio: Merrill Publishing.

Kazdin, A. (1994). *Behavior Modification in Applied Settings.* Pacific Grove, California: Brooks/Cole Publishing.

Chapter 17

Miltenberger, R. (1997). *Behavior Modification: Principles and Practices.* Pacific Grove, California: Brooks/Cole Publishing.

Chapter 18

Abernathy, W. (1996). *The Sin of Wages.* PerfSys Press.

about the authors

....

Mary R. Burch, Ph.D., is a Certified Behavior Analyst. She has also been approved as a Certified Applied Animal Behaviorist by the Animal Behavior Society. Her behavioral research has been published by the U.S. Department of Education. Dr. Burch has trained dogs to the advanced levels of obedience and is considered a national expert on the topic of therapy dogs. She is the author of *Volunteering with Your Pet* and *The Border Collie,* published by Howell Book House. Dr. Burch has won the Maxwell Medallion from the Dog Writers' Association of America for her writing on dog-related topics. She is a founding member of the Animal Trainer's Forum in the Association for Behavior Analysis.

Jon S. Bailey, Ph.D., is a Professor of Psychology at Florida State University. Dr. Bailey is a Fellow of the American Psychological Association and was on the Board of Directors of the Society for the Experimental Analysis of Behavior. Dr. Bailey is a past editor of the *Journal of Applied Behavior Analysis,* and is the author of the book *Research Methods in Applied Behavior Analysis.* Dr. Bailey serves as an expert witness on behavioral issues.

index